FOREWORD BY FRANKLIN GRAHAM

On a and a WING PRAYER

THE (MOSTLY) **TRUE MISADVENTURES** OF AN **ALASKAN BUSH PILOT**

RALPH C. MELOON, JR.

Publishing support provided by
Ignite Press
5070 N. Sixth St. #189
Fresno, CA 93710
www.IgnitePress.us

ISBN: 979-8-9870269-0-8
ISBN: 979-8-9870269-1-5 (Hardcover)
ISBN: 979-8-9870269-2-2 (E-book)

For bulk purchase and for booking, contact:

Ralph Meloon, Jr.
ralphmeloon@gmail.com

Scripture quotations marked (NLT) are taken from the Holy Bible, New Living Translation, Copyright © 1996, 2004, 2015 by Tyndale House Foundation. Used by permission of Tyndale House Publishers, a Division of Tyndale House Ministries. All rights reserved.

Scriptures marked (KJV) are taken from the King James Version, public domain.

Library of Congress Control Number: 2022915908

Cover design by Liubov Bezpalova
Edited by Charlie Wormhoudt
Interior design by Eswari Kamireddy

FIRST EDITION

F1

To all my many friends and fellow pilots throughout the years who have helped me to learn more about flying–especially flying remote in all kinds of conditions–and who have assisted me in recovery of bent airplanes, such as Dr. Alex Russell, Tom Dwinell, Rich Dykema, Roger Rupp, Mark Lang, OHOP pilots John Erickson and Bill Simms, Pierce Basset, Danny Herman, Glen Alsworth, B Alsworth, Franklin Graham, Rocky McElveen, Jeremy Davis, his father John Davis, Dave Wilder, the whole MARC (Missionary Aviation Repair Center) family, especially Roald Amundsen. And to a very special mother who, hearing I was still flying with a runout engine nearly a thousand hours over recommended overhaul, sent me a check to buy a new one. And above all, to my Lord and Savior Jesus Christ, who died on a cross some 2,000 years ago to pay the penalty for my sins, and who kept me safe through all these adventures.

Thank you.

Acknowledgments

My wife Wanda (Wendi) Meloon for enduring the many questions and long hours, giving great advice along the way.

My daughters Tanya Provost, Heather Morning, and, especially, Lisa Rassi who gave suggestions for title and content.

Franklin Graham for his encouragement, valuable suggestions, and persistence in seeing me through to the end.

CONTENTS

FOREWORD

I 've known Ralph Meloon for over 30 years. The stories that you're about to read will take you on an epic adventure of flying in the Alaskan bush. They showcase the raw beauty and ruggedness of this Great Land, and also the challenges of dealing with ever-changing weather, difficult terrain, cargo, and people who don't often appreciate the danger you put yourself in as an Alaskan pilot.

Some may question the truthfulness of Ralph's "misadventures" as he calls them, but let me tell you—I've lived through some of these escapades and they are accurately told. Ralph is not only an excellent pilot, but an incredible hunter. For those of us who are pilots and love the allure of the outdoors, these tales will get your juices going.

The problem with this book is once you begin, you won't want to put it down. So don't get started until you have time to sit and enjoy *On a Wing and a Prayer: The (Mostly) True Misadventures of an Alaska Bush Pilot.* It's a great read.

Franklin Graham, President and CEO
Samaritan's Purse
Billy Graham Evangelistic Association

INTRODUCTION

BEGINNINGS

I first saw Alaska on a family vacation when I was 17. It was a grueling 6,000-mile trip. We drove a Chevrolet station wagon and loaded it with camping gear that we used every day. My sister, Marion, did not go along, but my brother Ken, along with Mother and Dad and I, set course for Alaska. We had lots of adventures along the way, from having to negotiate a railroad trestle several hundred feet above the Peace River in British Columbia with one wheel between the rails and one outside near the edge with no siding, to surviving nearly a dozen flat tires from the terrible gravel road called the Alcan (short for Alaska-Canadian) Highway, to my being chased by an inebriated Native with what appeared to be a tomahawk in Whitehorse, Yukon.

When we arrived at the Alaskan border separating the new 49th state of America and the Canadian Yukon Territories, to my mind it might as well have been heaven. I was hooked. The year was 1959. Alaska was just a baby, having been brought into the

Yours truly Ralph Jr., my father Ralph Sr., and my mother Betty R. Meloon

Union officially by Congress in late 1958, but only formalized as a state when signed by President Dwight Eisenhower on January 3, 1959. For sure I was coming back someday.

Sometime in the early seventies I became enthused with flying as a means of promoting my business. My enthusiasm was so high I ended up teaching the ground school within several months of taking it myself. I didn't stop with my private pilot's license. I went on to acquire an IFR (instrument flight rules) rating, allowing me to fly in most weather conditions, then a multi-engine rating, and eventually a commercial rating. I bought my first airplane, a small single-engine with retractable gear and I quickly advanced to a twin engine.

When the gas crunch hit hard in the early seventies, I sold the twin and bought a high-performance, single-engine turbo, a Cessna T 210. I set out almost immediately for Alaska from Indiana. By the time I arrived in Edmonton, Canada, all the radios had ceased working. One of the FBOs (fixed base operators) there worked on it, and I thought it was fixed.

Not so. After flying for an hour between layers somewhere north of the Alcan Highway between Fort Nelson and Watson Lake, I realized my navigational equipment had ceased working. I had been flying I was not sure how long following an instrument that was not working. I panicked. One can't make major navigational mistakes in country like that and expect to survive. I had no idea how far off course I might have wandered.

It was then I noticed off my left wing about ten miles away what appeared to be an airstrip in the middle of nowhere. The lower layer was beginning to break up, and I headed straight for the strip. I was so thrilled I turned on final without even doing a flyover and was preparing to land when I realized the strip was deserted and had tall weeds on it. I didn't care. I was landing no matter what.

I almost went on my back in the soft material, which was caused by the frost melting in May. I was stuck in the muck. I got out and observed lots of bear tracks. I grabbed my gun and began walking around. A lopsided sign hanging on the side of a dilapidated hangar read "Canadian Department of Defense."

I headed toward a cabin I spotted in the woods and pushed open the door. It was surprisingly clean and looked like it had been used within the last year. I found a map with a trail marked with an X, probably for where I stood. It put me 30 miles north of the Alcan Highway, above the Liard River and alongside the Coal River. I breathed a sigh of relief.

I now had an idea where I was, but would have to spend the night, and hopefully in the coolness of the early morning hours while the ground was still firm, I could get the plane moving and make a departure. The takeoff went well, and I proceeded to Alaska.

I spent several days flying around the state and finally landed in a small town called Soldotna on the Kenai Peninsula to refuel before striking out across the treacherous Gulf of Alaska for Ketchikan. A sign on a hangar there read "MARC: Missionary Aviation Repair Center." I went in and paid my bill and met Roald and Harriet Amundsen, missionaries for 20 years in Nome, Alaska, and now called to serve in this aviation-oriented capacity.

Eventually I would make this place my home, and their oldest son, John, would build my house along with his brother, Tim, who was an electronics whiz. In the years following, Roald and Harriet would become like a mother and father away from home for me.

With the plane serviced, I took off and crossed the Gulf of Alaska to Ketchikan. After fueling, I continued through Canada and back to Indiana. But something had changed inside me.

The years flew by with me back and forth between Alaska and the lower 48.

Even though I had a cabin on the Kenai River as early as 1975, and a permanent home built in 1980 (also on the Kenai River, but in the City of Soldotna) I was still flying back and forth to the lower 48 on business. But by 1989, with my ears humming from the screech of tires and the almost constant wailing of sirens from police and emergency vehicles, my nose irritated by the smell of burning rubber from tires spinning out, and my eyes reeling from observing the obscene gestures of impatient drivers, I decided to call it quits. I sold my interests in my businesses there.

Bush flying in Alaska can be an incredible out of this world experience one moment and sheer terror the next. That combination of beauty and terror is what I wish to give you a sample of in the pages of this book. While you likely aren't an Alaskan bush pilot and you may never see Alaska (though I hope you will), these stories of adventure, lessons learned, and flying on a wing and a prayer will give you a taste of adventure from the comfort of your home.

This book will glue you to your chair, causing you to be keenly aware of our human frailty and need to depend on others—especially God—to navigate the sometimes treacherous paths our life's journeys take us on. My hope and prayer is that by reading this recollection of some of my adventures and dealings along my life's journey and how I coped with them, you will be inspired to step out in faith and experience all that your life offers you, receiving the charge like Joshua: ". . . Be strong and of good courage. Be not afraid. Neither be thou dismayed. For the Lord thy God will be with thee whithersoever thou goest" (Joshua 1:9, KJV).

CHAPTER 1

UPSIDE DOWN ON THE TAYLORS

When I woke and crawled out of my tarp, what I saw was like a nightmare. What had been a manageable Alaskan bush "incident" had turned into a major event. It seemed surreal. The landscape before me was strewn with aircraft parts for a hundred yards or so, with one wing off the ridge lying several hundred feet below.

I made my way to what was left of the main fuselage and squeezed in upside down. I found the radio, switched on the master (the main electrical switch), and with the last dying power began transmitting on the emergency frequency 121.5: "Mayday, mayday."

I peeked up out of the plane and noticed the high contrail of a jet passing overhead. Suddenly my radio crackled to life, and I heard a voice in broken English say, "This is JAL 747 reading you loud and clear."

Excitedly I keyed my mike and announced I had a slight problem below and needed help. The voice came back and asked if I wanted to "declare emergency" and have them "call FAA."

I said, "Just a minor problem, no injury. Would you call Dick

Page of Soldotna, Alaska, and tell him Ralph Meloon needs help on the west side of the Taylors?" I knew Dick's number by heart and said it several times and then lost them. Dick had flown and hunted with me in the area and knew it well. If only the Japanese fellow understood and made the call, I would receive some help fairly soon.

That fateful morning the sky was ablaze with red. That old adage, "Red sky in the morning, sailors take warning," applies to bush pilots as well. There was a fast-approaching, played-out typhoon from Japan making its way across the state. Often these huge weather systems would stall out over Alaska and eat the state for several days to a week or so.

It had been several days since I had successfully moved a hunting party of five men—most if not all of them board members of Focus on the Family—and all their personal gear to the west side of the famous Taylor Mountains in south-central Alaska. The precipitous ridge I set them on was loaded with caribou bulls. Their bulging necks and huge racks spoke volumes about their readiness to do battle over the many cows. Landing on the rocky, uneven ridge right in their midst was a challenge for even the most seasoned bush pilot. At this point in my bush flying experience, I was definitely pushing the envelope, flying off a tiny island on the river to this ridge spilling off the west side of the Taylors.

Putting aside the daunting challenge of just becoming familiar with the remote terrain and trying to judge unknown places for safe operations, one has to contend with the unpredictability of weather. The warmer Japanese current flowing north clashes with the frigid Alaskan water, causing huge weather fronts loaded with wind.

The day I went to retrieve the hunting party it was this factor sending chills up and down my spine as I prepared the plane for flying. My Piper Super Cub was positioned downriver about a mile from the main camp. By the time I had fueled my plane, crawled in, and cranked up, the wind on the river had increased to over ten knots. Tension built in me as I wondered what was happening up on the mountain. I was certain they hadn't begun to break down camp, much less ready trophies.

As I approached, I could see I had my work cut out for me. The improvised "wind sock," a piece of orange ribbon tied to a bush, was wildly dancing in a brisk wind, though holding steady one way—a good sign. Looking south, I could see lowering clouds moving our way. The hunters saw me and waved as I flew over and prepared to land.

Downed animals were scattered here and there in various stages of being field dressed. I swung around, made my approach, landed, and stopped within 50 feet with the slight uphill and stiff headwind. I hopped out and explained what was coming and that they needed to hustle and finish preparing their trophies and break camp. There wasn't a moment to spare.

I began loading the plane while the hunters broke camp. I made my first takeoff roll from where I had stopped. Turning around to taxi back to gain a little extra space was not an option under the circumstances. It was going to be a hard, long, and intense several hours of shuttle. The wind seemed to pick up with each passing moment. Blowing maybe 15 to 20 knots and quartering off my left wing, it necessitated tying the rack or racks on one side to help against the wind.

I quickly left with the first hunter and his belongings and a little meat from the kills. The plane flew right off. I returned and kept shuttling, sometimes just meat and belongings and racks. The wind kept increasing throughout the day and was becoming more erratic, dancing about.

I had now moved all the hunters down to the island along with their belongings and trophies. I lacked only a couple racks and the final meat pile. I was bound and determined to yard that final load off the mountain.

I took off, fighting the controls in the increasing winds on the river to fly up on the ridge to finish. The orange ribbon was whipping about wildly now. I lined up to land, wrestling the controls like never before. A downdraft sucked me suddenly toward a jagged outcropping of rocks. I immediately responded with full power to catch my descent. The plane recovered with the extra power, despite more rocking and rolling, and I made a not so pretty landing.

I jumped out, threw the meat into the back of the plane, and quickly bungee strapped the remaining racks to the left strut. Suddenly, a gust of wind began to lift my plane and fly it backward off the hill. I jumped on the right strut and held on and prayed.

It came to a rest about 30 feet back with me still straddling the strut and now shaking like a leaf. For a moment I caught a break as the gusts died down, and I leaped for the cockpit and frantically began cranking the engine. It fired, and I applied full power.

The quartering crosswind had now swung to the opposite side. The plane began to lurch uncontrollably. I was flying almost sideways along the ridge. Try as I may, I could not outclimb the increasing terrain. A rising ridge snagged me in an instant, and down I came in a heap of smashed wing tips.

I turned off the mags (magnetos, which provide the spark to the sparkplugs], to prevent a fire and crawled out. I had a blue tarp, which I grabbed and headed for an alder patch. The rain now was raking the ridge in savage sheets so heavy I thought the seventh vial of Revelation was happening. I had a handheld wind gauge that showed winds at 40 knots and gusting. The washed-out typhoon was spending its energy square on the Taylor Mountains. I wrapped up in the tarp to survive the night and tried to sleep. The gusts became so wicked I was sure they were going to blow me out of the alders.

Then I heard it. A sickening thud and then another. My little plane was being lifted and tumbled like tumbleweeds in the storm's fury. It was the worst night of my life up to that point.

The next day the wind continued to blow. I was hungry. I took out my survival knife, which thankfully I held onto, and began carving off a piece of raw, stinky caribou meat. Because it was from the bulls' deepest rut, it was strong. Because of the loads I would be carrying, I had stripped my plane of guns and most survival gear. That was a mistake. When I needed that stuff the most, I had little to nothing. I now wished I'd bagged this final flight, secured my plane on that tiny island, and enjoyed the camaraderie of a night around a warm campfire with the hunters.

It was then, to my utter dismay, that my eye caught movement. Three brown bears headed straight for me. I slowly backed away from the doomed plane and headed downhill, away from the bears. I remember seeing a movie once starring Anthony Hopkins where he survived a plane crash and was stranded in the Alaskan wilderness with a blood-thirsty brown bear menacingly hunting him down. All he had to defend himself was a knife. The meat, which I knew they would be attracted to, was downwind from them, but it wouldn't be for long on their present course, and my supply of survival food would shortly be claimed by this large sow and her two nearly-grown three-year-old cubs.

I found a group of alders to hide in. It was going to be another long night of anxiously waiting for help. With the new threat of bears in the immediate area, I was concerned. I took my survival knife out, cut a large alder branch off, and using my shoelaces, attached the knife to it, forming a makeshift spear. My tarp was still up in the bushes where I had slept the night before and too near the bears for my comfort to try and retrieve. The rain began to fall again. I fashioned a bed of soft tundra under the alders. Exhausted and discouraged, I tried resting.

Many thoughts raced through my mind, but I thankfully was mindful of the fact God had this. He knew and cared and had a lesson for me. Help would soon arrive.

Early in the dawning light, I was awakened by nearby scraping in the brush. I sat up and reached for my makeshift spear. Had the bears found me? I saw movement through the alders and a flash of brown. Were my eyes playing tricks on me? I remained motionless. I knew I smelled like caribou, and the bear's keen scent would be zeroing in on me. But also the human scent would be there, and most wild bears tend to run rather than confront a human.

Suddenly another sound pierced the quietness. Far off at first but something. My heart began to pound. Was it a plane? Closer and closer it came. Yes, it was, and descending fast.

I slowly stood and looked around. Whoever it was must have seen the wreckage. I ran out of the alders to get a better look and saw the bears scrambling uphill with that little Super Cub in hot pursuit. The plane veered off and began circling. Sure enough, it was my friend from Red Devil, Dangerous Dan himself. Either Rocky had made it to Red Devil or the 747 pilot had done his job. Regardless, help had arrived and just in time.

Danny then flew low and slow over me and wagged his wings while dropping a package. It was food and a note. The note asked if I wanted him to call RCC (Rescue Command Center) in Anchorage and arrange for a rescue, which meant the FAA would be involved, or did I want to hike the five miles down to the river and be picked up by a passing boat?

There was a third option. It involved a pilot in Red Devil who had bought one of my old Super Cubs. He knew me and said he would be willing to help, but if it meant flying out there and landing, he wanted to be sure I marked off a better place to land. Not having a working radio, we had to communicate with hand signals.

I signaled to have the fellow fly out, and I would take some orange ribbon, which I always carried in my plane, to mark out a good landing spot lower down. With that, Dan flew off toward Red Devil and I proceeded downhill to find a flatter spot, on which it would be easier to land. It turned out to be a mile away, and seeing it I wished I had dropped my party there instead of that craggy ridge and let them do some walking for the caribou. Lessons learned.

With food in my tummy and spear in hand, I waited for the sound of another plane.

Later that afternoon, with the wind calmed down to about 15 knots, I heard an aircraft approaching, and sure enough it was one of my old white with red-and-blue trim Super Cubs. The pilot found me and noted my ribbon markings and the stick I held with a "windsock" marker attached. He lined up and tentatively landed, overshooting a ways, but nevertheless making an uneventful landing. He got out, relieved himself and suggested I fly them out of there.

He even offered to lend me his plane to use to fly parts up to my plane and rescue it. I thanked him for that and assured him if I messed up, he would be reimbursed.

Apparently the previous night, my comrade and confidant Rocky McElveen knew I hadn't returned and had scrambled a boat from our main camp and headed downriver to Red Devil, some 100 miles or so by water in the dark to get help. This was a harrowing accomplishment.

We left promptly and headed back to Red Devil. After making arrangements to get all our hunters out and down to Red Devil to coordinate a flight back to Anchorage, I jumped in my Cessna P210 parked at Red Devil and headed back to Soldotna to get the parts I needed to fix my broken plane. Never in a million years would I have believed that in less than ten days I would be flying that crippled plane off the Taylors.

CHAPTER 2

UPSIDE DOWN IN A SWAMP

It was a little less than an hour flight in a Super Cub from where we were on the Taylor Mountains to Red Devil. Kim, a very capable missionary mechanic with MARC who was assisting in the recovery of my plane, bravely got in behind me as I prepared for the tentative departure. I knew we would be close on fuel. When we were just past the halfway mark, the engine sputtered. I quickly switched to the right tank. The engine coughed once and then smoothed out. We were now on our last reserves. I could faintly see in the distance the glimmer of lights at Sleetmute off to my two o'clock position. Red Devil was hidden by Barometer Mountain.

The cockpit was dark. It was now oh-dark-thirty outside. I had no battery power. I didn't even have a flashlight. I had grown too familiar with the area and had become complacent. Though remote, once one flies an area so long, it tends to become less daunting. But this was nighttime flying over hostile country filled with many obstacles and bears.

As we passed over my homestead some 35 miles up the Holitna River from the Kuskokwim, I was wishing I had a lighted runway.

Though short by normal standards, it was about 600 feet usable, plenty for a bush plane, though narrow with obstructions on each end. There were fox dens at about the halfway point one had to be careful to avoid. I kept on my heading.

Roger Rupp, who operated off his own private airstrip in Soldotna and had an aircraft shop to work on planes, had flown his own bush plane out to assist—but since we couldn't talk to them by radio, I had no idea that he took off right after me.

Then it happened. The engine sputtered again, only this time it went totally silent. I switched back to the other tank and nothing. I checked the mags, and they were still on. Kim behind me was panicking. We were at approximately 2,500 feet, though it was hard to tell in the darkness.

I could see a lighter area below us. I figured it was open, swampy tundra and began slowly circling as we descended. Having no lights inside to watch the altimeter didn't help. Unable to turn landing lights on near the ground didn't help either.

I could imagine Kim behind me was turning green, one of a pilot's worst nightmares. When I sensed the ground was close, I could see an area growing darker ahead. Were we nearing trees? I was too low to try any last-second maneuvers, so I held course. As it grew darker ahead, I felt I had some extra airspeed and needed to bleed it off to crash as slow as possible, but I knew not where.

I started pulling back on the stick. Whatever it was ahead, I managed to clear it. Now I was over a lighter spot again and bleeding off airspeed fast. I felt the plane shuttering like it does just before a stall. I pulled on full flaps and figured this was it. Slow down, little plane, I thought to myself. I was flying solely by feel. The plane lurched slightly one way then another as the wings made contact with some dead swamp spruce. Then the tires touched terra firma.

We bounced and flipped, ending upside down in a small body of water. I turned the mags off and felt my head getting damp from the water. I knew we had to get out of there, as I had no idea how deep it was. We unhooked our seatbelts and fell into the water. I had already  opened the door, and we quickly rolled out, wet and cold.

It turned out to be about three to four feet of water. We slogged through it to a dry, wooded raised area and pulled ourselves up. We were shivering. We heard another plane flying high overhead and figured it was Roger, who had no idea the detour we had just taken. Hopefully, when he realized we had not landed, he would let Dangerous Dan know, and he would come looking for us.

Fortunately, we had a lighter and quickly gathered some wood and got a roaring fire going. We had a small tarp and huddled under it, allowing the heat from the fire to seep in and dry us out.

We awoke with a white blanket of snow covering us. We were shivering. We gathered more wood and rebuilt the fire and waited. I knew the Holitna River was east, and we could head that way for sure. Then we heard it. A plane was coming straight to us. It was Dangerous Dan again.

No sooner had he emerged from behind Barometer Mountain than he saw the smoke of our fire and figured it was us. He had already prepared a supply package, which he dropped with a map. He circled an area on a map where he thought we were and asked us to signal by waving if we wanted to walk out; otherwise, he would call RCC (Rescue Command Center). That was the last thing I wanted.

My wife had called Danny to check on my progress, and when I had not arrived, she became alarmed. She asked Danny to go looking for us ASAP in the morning. Danny said I probably had landed at the homestead. Clearly, we hadn't.

We waved our answer, put out the fire, then took up a heading toward the river and began hiking. It was cold and dreary. It snowed on and off. Twice we had to strip and hold our clothes over our heads and cross streams. This was not a fun hike. A couple of times I think Kim just wanted to give up. We stopped and built a fire to warm ourselves.

As we neared the river, we heard a chainsaw. When we could see the river, we noticed a Native sawing his wood for winter. We shouted, but he couldn't hear us. We waited until he set the chainsaw down and yelled. He looked our way, got into his boat, and came across to pick us up. He was very kind.

We told him what happened, and he took us downriver to the village. The local school teacher gave us some of her husband's clothes to wear while she dried ours. I called Dangerous Dan at the hardware store in Red Devil and told him we had made it out and asked if he would mind coming to pick us up.

Within an hour both he and Mac—a fellow villager bush pilot with a reputation with whom I had no acquaintance—arrived from Red Devil in their planes, Danny in his Piper Super Cub and Mac in his Piper Super Cruiser. I think Mac had a few drinks under his belt. Danny appeared his usual self. Kim and I drew straws as to who would ride with Danny and who with Mac. He got Danny and I pulled Mac.

As far as I knew, Danny had never gotten a pilot's license. He told me once when he flew off the gold mining strip of Wild Bill over near Two Lakes, he saw a bear up a ravine and decided to turn left and fly up to see it. Only problem was he was too low and too loaded to outclimb the terrain and ended up in a tree, dangling like a broken kite. The bear decided to take a look, and if it hadn't been for the fact that brown bears can't climb trees well (kind of like lions), he might have become dinner that evening.

Fortunately for Danny he happened to have an ELT on board, which alerted RCC in Anchorage after a satellite passing overhead pinpointed where he was for a rescue. The other fortunate thing was because he didn't have a pilot's license the FAA could take from him, he wouldn't lose it.

Back to our current situation: my pilot was an unknown to me. It was only eight miles downriver to Red Devil, but those were the longest eight miles I have ever experienced flying. At least twice Mac dove and swooped around and toward Danny, narrowly missing him. One time he went head on at him, playing chicken. I could see the whites of Kim's eyes behind Danny, who was biting his lip and holding course hoping for a flyby. It seemed Mac was determined to show me what a great pilot he was, doing loops and stalls. I had always wanted to do aerobatics, but not with Mac.

Danny landed and taxied up to the store.

I finally reached in my wallet and waved a 100-dollar bill in his face, begging him to land. That did it. He landed promptly. I was shaking so bad I couldn't stand and ended up half crawling to the hardware store from the plane.

Kim said later that Danny looked out and saw me coming and commented: "Look at Ralph. He just had his first ride with Mac." I understand that not long after getting back home, Kim, who was relatively new to Alaska, decided to leave and not return.

I understand that sometime later Mac tried numerous times to find a way through the mountains in bad weather and ended up in Talkeetna refueling. After falling off his plane twice trying to refuel while inebriated, the local FBO called the FAA and turned him in. He was arrested on the spot. It probably saved his life, at least for the time being. One doesn't drink and fly.

CHAPTER 3

RESCUE (PHASE ONE)

I t was now the middle of October in Alaska, and the snow was beginning to fall pretty regularly. There had not been any hard freezes yet, and timing was critical to get back to the site of the Super Cub in the swamp to set it back on its wheels so it would freeze on top of the ice right side up and not in the ice upside down. The only way to salvage it, short of an expensive helicopter hire, was to right it on its tires before a hard, prolonged freeze then come back, take the tires off, put skis on, and fly it out of that small swamp.

I was pretty sure I could make it light on gas and no load, but I would have to cut down a few swamp spruce to prevent further damage. I still didn't know if I would have to bring another $3,000 propeller. I knew the windshield was split again, but I figured we could bring a battery-powered drill, make holes on each side of the crack and use wire to lace it together after we had applied some silicone Goop.

At another time with my Beaver, I let slip the front quarter of a moose while loading, and its hoof broke through the windshield. The resulting crack made my plane unairworthy. One cannot fly with a broken windshield. It would be dangerous, as well as not fly-able. In that case I had a tube of Goop and applied it to the outside and inside of the crack. I waited a couple of hours until it bonded, and then I took off. It held perfectly, and I didn't change that windshield until the next annual, which in my case didn't always mean one year.

I tried to find someone that would lend me a Super Cub on floats so I could attempt to land on one of several small beaver ponds just outside of the swamp where my plane was stranded. I believed I could touch down on the edge of the largest one and stop in time. They were all small potholes. If I didn't get stopped, my hope was that the weedy area between the ponds contained enough water that if I did overshoot, I would not hurt anything, and I could just power on to the next pond.

Since I had traded off my one Super Cub on floats for the Beaver floats, I did not have one. Try as I may, I could not find anyone who would lend me one, either because they didn't trust me or they had other uses at the time for their planes—probably the former. That left my Beaver on floats as my only choice. I had not seen any water close by in the area that looked long enough to safely land. I decided to overfly again and evaluate.

About three miles away, I found a fairly long, narrow beaver pond with a dam on one end that was the only real candidate. I got the necessary ropes and tools together and worked a trade arrangement with a close friend, Rich Dykema, to fly several of his hunters for caribou, and in trade he would help me rescue my Cub.

I had no idea what I was getting into. The next thing I know, Rich and I are in my Beaver with three of his hunters behind us and all of their gear. We were out somewhere between the Stuyahok and the Nushagak Rivers trying to find a pond we could land on near a migration of caribou. Finally we found what we were looking for: caribou, and lots of them, near a pond.

However, the pond was tiny, one we call a 40-mile-per-hour pond, meaning unless a wind of at least that speed was blowing, it was senseless to try landing, much less taking off. That country is known for how it blows, and it so happened that it was blowing that day.

We lined up into the wind and touched down. We overshot the end of the pond, ending up on shore by several feet. It took all five of us pushing, grunting, and shoving to get the big plane floating again. Now to take off was a whole other proposition.

At least we were light, but Rich had a worried look and asked as we turned into the wind, "Do you think we can make it?"

Without hesitation, I answered, "Pray."

As I poured the coals to it, I noticed out of the corner of my eye Rich with his head bowed. Voila. Our prayers were answered. We made it and turned north to head to our camp on the Holitna River near the Taylor Mountains.

It was oh-dark-thirty when we arrived, and in the moonlight we lowered over the river and set down just upriver from our camp, turned into the slough and parked. We built a roaring fire, cooked up some grub, and relaxed while sharing the adventures of the day.

It was sometime after this that Rich was missing something and went over to the airplane to look for it in the float compartments. He didn't find what he was looking for, but he did find something else, a heavy box marked bullets. He brought it over and showed it to me, telling me he was sure these were the bullets for the fellows we dropped off as they were using the same caliber guns and had packed them separately in the packaging required by airline security.

We now were convinced they were in the middle of the caribou migration with guns galore but no bullets. After the harrowing experience we'd just had, no way were we going back in there to give them their bullets that night, so we wrapped some thick brush around the box and duct taped it. We then tied an orange ribbon all around, leaving some to dangle for a marker. We decided the next morning we would just fly back, pass over their camp low and slow, then bombs away.

Sure enough, when we arrived the caribou were everywhere around them, even in their camp. It was like a petting zoo. The hunters were standing around appearing frustrated until they saw us. We made the drop successfully and left. We knew getting them out of there later would be a major project, especially with early freeze-up, but that would not happen until after we had finished phase one of the Cub rescue.

With that out of the way, we flew north to my homestead to make final preparations to fly my Beaver and land on the beaver pond to put us within striking distance of the Cub. We flew a heading several times from the beaver pond down to the Cub which turned out to be 210 degrees. We also estimated the distance as three miles and guessed how long it would take us to hike through the tundra to arrive at or near enough to begin searching. It was like hunting a needle in a haystack.

The landing with my DHC-2 Beaver on that tiny beaver pond could have been slower and shorter since I ended up banging into the beaver dam on the other end, knocking it out and causing water to escape. That wouldn't help when it came to our departure, so we spent several hours rebuilding the dam before proceeding on our hike to find the Cub.

I tied one orange ribbon about halfway there as we progressed. I probably should have tied more, though trees and brush in that part of the country were sparse. We set our watches, and at about the time we guessed we should have arrived, we came to a small, forested hill that looked familiar. Sure enough, we walked about 50 yards north, and there it was.

After righting it on its wheels, we pulled the swamp grass and mud out of the cowling, checked the propeller—pulling it through and watching it track—then drilled holes along the crack in the windshield and wired it together after spreading Goop on both sides. This repair worked excellent for ferrying, and in fact worked well for quite a while after the plane was rebuilt.

We then cut some logs with a bow saw, and using a longer log for a lever, we lifted up one side and then the other, placing small log rafts tied together under the tires to keep the wheels above the water level. There was no need to tie the plane down since the wind could not build up in that small swamp.

We began our hike back to the beaver pond. We had planned to fly to the homestead nearby before dark; my wife had hot chili going on the stove. However, that wasn't going to happen. Though we took the reciprocal heading and followed it closely (we thought) we missed where the plane was parked. We found a similar pond, and thought for sure it was the right one, but no plane. We ended up having to build a fire to stay warm while huddling together that night.

The next day we began looking again, even contemplating trying to go back to the Cub and start over, but instead we just kept wandering around in circles with no luck. It seemed we each would have a different idea which way to go, but to no avail. The country was too flat and the trees too short to climb and see anything.

I remember praying and asking God for direction and setting out on a more northerly course in the direction I believed would take us there. If I was right, somewhere along the way I would have to angle to the reciprocal heading that we took to get there, or 30 degrees. Where that was, I didn't know, but God did. Within 30 minutes of hiking on this course, we broke into a clearing that looked vaguely familiar. Could this be the place I'd tied the orange ribbon? I turned and looked both ways and thought I saw something a ways down the swamp.

Bingo. There was that orange ribbon tied to the one bush in the swamp. We were ecstatic. We turned to a 30-degree heading and set off, and within an hour or so we walked right to the beaver pond and saw our plane. We had camped less than a couple hundred feet from the right pond. It might as well have been a mile.

There was still enough light to depart. The pond had refilled adequately. We climbed in and taxied to the end of the swamp and shut down. It was so narrow there was no room to taxi turn. We got out, turned the plane, got back in, and powered up.

We made it with some to spare, heading over to the homestead nearby to get some grub and to prepare for the flight south to pick up Rich's hunters, their camp, and hopefully trophies.

CHAPTER 4

RESCUE (PHASE TWO)

The phone rang. It was Dangerous Dan from Red Devil. He informed me it had turned cold a couple weeks prior, and the thermometer had not risen above zero for at least a week of steady 20 below. The ponds near them were frozen with at least six to eight inches of ice, the Kuskokwim had huge floating ice pans beginning to jam up, and in places the river was frozen across. He thought I should have no problem landing on any pond out in that country.

I thanked him and called my friend, Pierce Bassett of Kenai. I had asked him earlier if he would accompany me in this last phase of rescue, and he readily agreed. He was one of the old-time Alaskan bush pilots with lots of experience and a yearning for adventure. The goggles and silk scarf fit this man to a tee.

We loaded my C-185, equipped with hydraulic wheel skis, with survival gear, extra rope, snowshoes, the straight skis for my Cub with bungees and springs, a couple five-gallon cans of gas, wing covers for both planes, and, engine covers with propane heaters. We topped off the plane and headed out with a fair-weather forecast, clear and cold.

We soon were through Merrill Pass and heading for my

homestead, which was quite close to where the Cub was situated. When we got to the Holitna River, ice pans covered most of the river, and they were moving slowly.

We headed to the landing spot and overflew it several times. A layer of snow covered the three ponds as well as in between them. We both agreed it would be best to leave the wheels down and land on the ice as close as we could to the near edge and brake slightly, pumping the brakes to try and stop within the small pond.

I did fairly well, but either not well enough or the pond was smaller than it looked. When we hadn't stopped by the opposite side, we began to enter the weeded area between the ponds, and the landing went totally south. As we continued to slow, we began breaking through and sinking. I slammed full power to the throttle while Pierce frantically pumped on the ski handle, trying to put the skis down and bring up the tires above the ski bottoms. But it was too late. We began sinking.

Fortunately, the left tire and ski got hung up part way down on a huge tundra bump. That was the good news. The bad news was that the right side sank out of sight, and the wing was in the water along with that side of the fuselage. The only thing we could think happened was that swamp gas (methane) was probably emitted in that area, and because lots of snow had accumulated among the weeds, it acted as an insulated blanket, keeping the hard freeze from happening.

Also, If I had it to do over, I would have touched down in the weedy area before the pond, which would have slowed me a lot and probably allowed me to get stopped within the boundary of the pond. Better, I might have pumped the skis down and landed on them and skied across the pond and the weedy area, keeping my speed up.

But this is all second-guessing. It is part of the learning experience called The School of Hard Knocks. But this is a tough school

to go to at 20 below zero Fahrenheit, and now we had to get a broken Cub to rescue the C-185. What a turn of events.

When we exited the plane, we both had to do it on the driver's
side, which was above water. When we stepped down, we realized
quickly that we had to use our snowshoes to spread our weight or
this was not going to end well. We put them out on the soft, soggy
snow and gingerly stepped down. It worked.

We then unloaded the skis for the Cub and the gas cans. We secured them to the skis after tying the skis together and began walking toward the forested area, which hid the Cub from the small
swamp on the other side. We stopped and rested and looked back
at the C-185 and began to formulate a plan and what tools we
would need.

We already had a small bottle jack to help remove the tires from
the Cub and replace them with the skis. But we needed something
better like a handyman jack. Also, we needed a couple chain saws to
cut logs to use in the rescue. That meant a trip to Red Devil in the
stranded Cub.

We noticed during the time we scurried about examining the
plane that the areas we had walked on with our snowshoes began
freezing. We decided to walk back and look again, and if this was
true, we would stomp out the area under the high wing and the
low wing where we could reach. We couldn't believe our eyes. Ice
was forming quickly, and if it would build thick enough to hold the
weight of jacks spread out on a log platform, we were in business.

We could walk ahead to the next beaver pond, knocking down
the weeds and bringing up the water to freeze solid, too. We were
beginning to feel optimistic. Now we had to rescue the Cub. The
temps were hovering in the zero-degree range.

We hiked through the woods and up to the Cub. We had brought
the heater and engine blanket, put them in place, and lit the propane stove to warm the engine while we worked cleaning the snow

off the wings. Then we had to wiggle the wings up and down and twist some, but the tires moved freely, and we were able to turn the little plane 180 degrees in the direction with the longest stretch of open ground and the fewest obstacles.

We then jacked up one side of the plane on the backside of the landing gear. We removed one tire at a time, zip-locked the brake cylinders and lines, and installed the skis. We emptied the two cans of gas all on the left side. We decided to give the heater more time to warm the motor and returned to the C-185 each carrying a tire and wheel.

We again spent more time stomping down the snow and weeds. We got out our survival gear, the tent and sleeping bags, and set up camp. With a bow saw and small ax, we cut logs for a fire. The days were so short now that with darkness coming, I probably would not make it back that night depending on how long it took to gather the necessary tools to free the Cessna from the ice and whatever other obstacle I might run into.

Pierce stayed put while I returned on snowshoes to the Cub to fly to Red Devil. I took my bow saw and went out on the path I had scoped out and cut several swamp spruce that would be in the way. After doing that, I removed the engine cover and threw it in the back of the plane along with the engine heater that had been under the cowling. I got in, switched the tank to left, primed it, turned on the mags, cracked the throttle ever so slightly, got back out, and, standing behind the propeller, grabbed a blade and pulled down.

Nothing. I did it again. Nothing. On the third try, however, the engine came to life. I reached in and pulled the throttle back as the plane was trying to inch forward on the ice. I jumped in quickly and got my feet on the rudder petals and shoved my heels down to brake. I let it warm up a bit until the temp gauge was beginning to move into the yellow.

This was it. I brought the throttle in full and the plane edged forward. The swamp was looking small. I had determined to head right for the tree line and at the very last moment pull back on the elevator while simultaneously pulling up on the flap handle. There would be no stopping, no second chance.

There were frozen tundra bumps and fallen trees frozen in the ground that I bumped and careened over while the tall trees ahead were approaching fast. I felt my tail getting lighter as I shoved the stick forward for feel. The trees were really close now in my face. There would be no second chance.

I let go of the throttle and grabbed the flap handle. I knew it would not be good to do this too soon, as it could hinder more than help. My timing had to be precise. If I didn't pull back on the elevator in the next couple seconds, it would be all over. I would crash into the trees at full speed. Pierce Basset would be left alone fending for himself. My family would have to be notified. A thousand thoughts raced through my mind.

I simultaneously pulled back on the elevator and the flap handle. I was off the ground now, literally climbing vertically up the tree line, half as high as the trees crowding my windshield were tall. I was high enough that at least the trees were getting thinner and were covered with more branches. I was running out of airspeed. I did not want to get behind the power curve. I needed to lower the nose some to gain some airspeed. But there wasn't room or time.

I was either going to clear the trees barely, stall out in the tops of them (which beat smashing headlong into them down low), or clear them by a hair's breadth. The little plane lurched slightly as I brushed the tops of the tree branches. Thankfully it kept flying. My heart was thumping hard, but I had made it. I breathed a prayer of thankfulness as I pointed my nose toward Barometer Mountain and Red Devil on the other side.

When I arrived at the runway paralleling the river and saw what I had done, my spirit of joy from the accomplishments so far began to turn somber. There was not one speck of snow on the runway. It was rocks, rocks, and more rocks. Whoever plowed the runway with the state grader did a great job for wheeled planes, but ski planes? Not so much.

I had no choice but to land. I knew my ski bottoms were about to suffer a grueling slide of destructiveness that would render them horribly disfigured on the bottoms. The only bright side was it would be a short slide. And short it was. I leaped out of the plane, grabbed the two empties, and hustled up to the hardware store.

Danny lent me everything I needed and filled my gas cans. We loaded it all into a trailer, and he hauled it down to my plane. I asked if he would help me throw some snow out in front of the plane and, using a jack, put some under the skis. He agreed. It didn't take long, and I was back in the Cub ready for Danny to hand-prop for me. It sure helped to have someone do the hand-propping while I worked the controls, especially on ice. Though it was dark now, there was a bright moon rising, so I decided to run back so we could start early the next morning.

I arrived over the ponds, dropped down and lined up to land, and almost forgot I was flying a very bent Cub that was barely flyable. I almost lost it on my turn when I slowed up. One wing tried to drop off, but I lowered the nose slightly and added power. I ended up going past the pond and into the middle area next to the Cessna but that was no problem as I had only straight skis. The Cub was much lighter, and the weedy area in between the ponds was freezing nicely due to Pierce having stomped a huge area for us to work on. By morning, I figured we should have several inches of ice to work with.

Pierce had a big fire going, and we melted snow and boiled the water to mix with the mountain pies we had brought along for survival. Mountain pie is lingo for dehydrated food that comes in many flavors. That night we had chili mac. The moon rose higher, and the air grew much colder. We were headed for a 30-below-zero night.

We put our heat blankets on the aircraft engines and lit the propane stoves. We crawled into our heavy down sleeping bags with air mattresses underneath. We only removed our bunny boots.

After a fitful night of tossing and turning, with the cold bone deep, we emerged from the tent to a warm-up of several degrees due to clouds moving in. With the clouds came a skiff of fresh snow. That meant we would need to put on our snowshoes and walk the area again.

We built up a roaring fire, heated some water for coffee, and discussed how we were going to tackle the task ahead so we could depart this bleak place. After much discussion, we decided to cut several six-foot logs and place them under each wing at the jack points. The low wing was the difficult one to start with, and of course we needed to chainsaw around its tip in the ice, and around the tail and part of the fuselage. Then of course the skis had to be cut around.

It was an arduous task, and working in cold like that it was slow going. But by mid-afternoon we were doing the initial jacking with the bottle jack on the low wing, little by little, bracing and jacking until finally we could get the handyman jack under. Now we could jack it level with the other side. At this point, we were ready to take turns jacking on one side, then the other, bracing, and cutting more timber to stack until we had the plane high enough that we could slip some longer logs under the skis and slowly let the plane down on them.

By this time we were exhausted and our daylight was gone. We were destined for at least one more night sleeping in the cold. It actually had warmed up a bit because of the cloud layer that had moved in and dropped snow. We slept quite well that night.

The next morning we rolled out of bed and put the final touches on our rescue. We removed the engine blanket and wing covers and propane heater. I entered the plane and proceeded to crank. It fired right off. I put the skis down, bringing the tires fully up. Now we were totally a ski plane. I taxied forward fairly fast for fear of falling through again, though I doubted it would happen as the area we stomped down seemed adequately frozen. I got to the next beaver pond and put the tires down again so I could brake some and made a fairly tight turn on the far edge of the second pond lining up for a future takeoff.

Then it happened. The engine sputtered and quit. I'd had the fuel valve selector set to feed on both tanks and now I realized it had run out of gas. Evidently in that position, with the low wing down so far, the fuel had siphoned completely out. I had to go to Red Devil anyway to refuel the Cub, but I dreaded going back and having to fool with that gravel runway on straight skis. Nevertheless, I had to return all the borrowed equipment.

Needless to say, I had to repeat the same scenario with the bent Cub landing on exposed gravel as they again had scraped the runway clean of the freshly fallen snow. I turned in the borrowed equipment and fueled up the Cub, plus a couple extra cans of fuel for the Cessna to make the trip to Red Devil. I got help again with shoveling snow under the skis and ahead of the plane for takeoff. I headed back to the Cessna to offload the 100LL aviation fuel and told Pierce I would wait for him there while he flew into Red Devil.

Finally, I could hear the Cessna coming back. I got in, cranked up, and waited for him to overfly to be sure it was the right plane. I then took off and joined him in the air for an uneventful flight back to civilization. Because the plane had been so severely damaged, I asked Pierce to fly throttled back and with some flaps so we could stay together.

When we entered the Chigmit Mountains, I held my breath when the turbulence began to buffet the plane. One has no idea just how bad the attachment points could be damaged. I found out on return and rebuilding the plane that one of the attachment points holding the main front spar on the left wing was cracked and could very likely have broken, ripping off the wing in flight had some moderate to severe turbulence been encountered.

I did climb up high in the mountains, like 9,000 feet, to stay out of channel terrain. I forgot to lean out the engine, whereupon it began running a bit rough, which got my attention. I mentioned it to Pierce, and he reminded me to lean the engine. I had already tried carb heat, but that was not the problem.

We began to let down over Cook Inlet into the Kenai/Soldotna area, and when we arrived at the Soldotna airport there wasn't a speck of snow anywhere. I had no choice but to land on the blacktop. I had Pierce land first, park, and direct traffic. When I came in low over several parked aircraft, I had a clear ramp ahead right in front of Missionary Aviation Repair Center. The ground slide was short—very short.

I had a lot of observers, but no one took a video. In those days folks didn't carry iPhones for fast video and pictures. That could be a good thing considering the FAA would have frowned on landing on the ramp. We used to take off from the ramp and not think much about it in those days. I got help to put wheel dollies under the skis and move the bent Cub to my parking spot nearby until I could work on it.

The work took all winter. The lessons learned and experiences gained from these early mishaps definitely shaped my flying for years to come.

The question has come up as to whether I would go through all that again to salvage a plane with all the risks, mainly of life and limb. I probably would not. But no one ever knows when starting such a project what it might turn into.

That is true of most endeavors in life.

CHAPTER 5
FLYING THE HOLITNA RIVER

The Holitna River is approximately 110 miles long. It flows northeasterly to join the Kuskokwim River (Alaska's second largest river system) near Sleetmute. Its headwaters are formed by three different streams: the Shotgun (the main source tributary), the Kogrukluk (meaning middle fork), and the Chukowan. This country lies above Dillingham, Alaska, and was a route traveled inland by Russian traders and others from Bristol Bay, navigating via a series of lakes stacked one on top of another until they reached the Holitna River system.

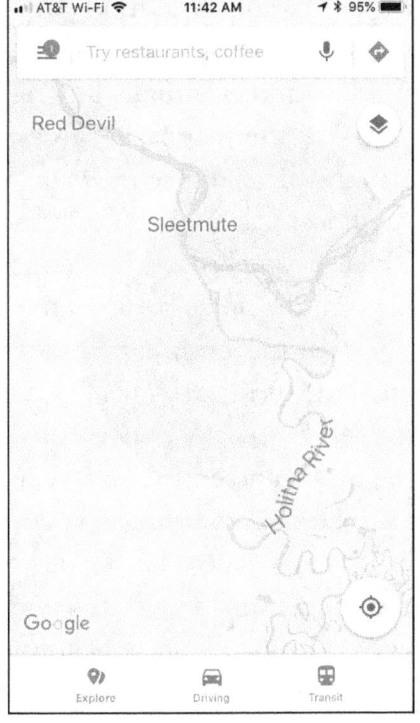

The Shotgun Hills, which lie south of the Taylor Mountains, are prime hunting grounds for grizzlies, black bear, moose, and caribou. The Holitna River system itself is a resource rich in salmon runs and several other species of fish such as shee fish, arctic grayling, and huge northern pike with voracious appetites.

I came into this country almost 40 years ago through the acquisition of a homestead some 35 miles upriver from Sleetmute. How that came about is a story unto itself. I was hunting mountain goat out of Seward, Alaska, on the Kenai Peninsula by boat. A sourdough (a seasoned Alaskan who has spent winters in Alaska) who lived in a cabin near the area had some peculiar traits. I heard tell he lassoed and hogtied a stallion—with the help of a few inebriated Natives in exchange for some hooch—and slid it down a ramp from a pickup truck into a 14-foot Zodiac raft with a 30 HP kicker. In the darkness, he motored many miles down Resurrection Bay, out around dangerous Cape Resurrection—exposed to the Gulf of Alaska—and eventually into his bay.

When he made the shore near his cabin, the mean horse had enough and clamped down on his arm and began shaking it violently, almost tearing it from his body. Only a .357 magnum revolver, which he packed on his hip, saved him the loss of his arm as he plugged the horse between the eyes.

I met this bushman, and we became somewhat friendly. He invited me to come by his place anytime. I decided to try landing on his beach with my Super Cub. I taxied up to a high point of land off the beach and ended up staying for the night.

The next morning I discovered that my plane had been eaten by his cows. After chasing off several bears in his garbage trailer, we used duct tape to piece the plane back together to make it flyable—barely. I took off straight towards the ocean with a slight onshore breeze and didn't make liftoff before hitting the water. That was when I realized these bush planes could actually run their wheels on water as long as there was just enough speed.

Later that month he showed up at my house in Soldotna with a proposition to sell me a homestead he had acquired on the Holitna River. I thought that was a novel idea. It was remote, had a little airstrip on it, was on the river itself, and even had a small building or two. The outhouse had only one wall—the back. Needless to say, the only spray needed when using that facility was mosquito spray and lots of it. The country was low and loaded with birds. It also was loaded with biting insects.

So we flew together in my Super Cub to the homestead's airstrip. It was a two-and-a-half-hour flight through Merrill Pass, one of Alaska's most challenging. I loved it. Being wild, remote, and with a fish on literally every cast, what was there not to like?

We flew to Red Devil and met folks there. I should have gotten a clue from their reaction to seeing him what might be in store for me. We nailed down a deal, I paid the price, and I had my own authentic Alaskan homestead. With it came a John Deere 350 dozer and a small Kubota tractor. The dozer was run up the river from Red Devil in February and several times broke through the ice and almost disappeared, requiring a rather rapid exit from the vehicle to wait and see if it dug itself out of the hole, which it did several times. Operating in this country, especially in the dead of winter, requires a lot of risk-taking and courage. I had no idea what I was getting into.

Over the years flying between Soldotna and the Holitna area, I experienced many adventures. I remember one flight with my dog, Trapper, a golden retriever, in the back seat. We had followed the Hoholitna River, which joined the Holitna just a few miles upriver from my place. It was a wonderful river system in its own right with Whitefish Lake as its headwaters. We left the Hoho where the

South Fork joined and proceeded across some of Alaska's best hunting grounds for the Mulchatna River, which flowed out of Turquoise Lake in route for Lake Clark pass—I had received word that Merrill Pass was down (choked with clouds and low to no visibility) and not flyable.

As I flew along, I saw a nice band of caribou and dropped lower to take a look. Wow. What I saw got my adrenaline running. Many trophy bulls were browsing along some small hills above a tiny lake. *Should I?* I thought to myself. I didn't think long and landed in a jiffy. It was landable, but was it takeoff-able? That was the question. I parked the plane, tailing it into the shore. I set camp and waited until early morning.

Trapper and I wound our way up into the hilly country and within a mile spotted some pretty big antlers dancing above the landscape. Excitedly I moved forward and positioned myself. Trapper was not a help. He knew what a gun did, and the noise bothered him. I finally pinpointed a nice trophy and dropped it.

Then the fun began—not really. I skinned it out, quartered it, took the backstraps and tenderloins and laid them on a tarp. While I worked on the neck meat, rib meat, and brisket, I noticed Trapper had disappeared. Forevermore, I thought.

Then I noticed a backstrap missing. I couldn't believe it. He had stolen it and was probably burying it somewhere. Then I saw him coming. I turned my back and pretended to be working and watched out of the corner of my eye. He picked up the other backstrap and headed back from where he had come, dragging it. I followed to see where he was burying it. I doubted he was that discriminating with his choice of meat. It was just all there was so far that he could actually pick up and carry.

When I discovered his hiding place, I scolded him, dug it up, and hauled it back. When I finished dressing it out, I had quite a haul. Back in those days I could pack most of it, but with the large rack, I decided to split it up into two loads. It took the rest of the daylight to get it moved to the plane. I don't think I could have flown out anyway late that afternoon as the wind was blowing pretty hard out of a small pass and there was crosswind on the small lake.

The next morning it was calm. I tied the rack on the float structure, loaded everything else in the Cub along with Trapper, and tried to take off. It was a bad idea. No way would that little plane haul all that weight on floats out of that small lake. It was just too small to make a step turn safely and have enough room in the longer stretch to make it out. On one attempt I shut down too late and ended up on shore a ways, and it took an hour or so with a small tree working the floats to get the plane back floating all the way.

I decided the only way was to drop a part of the meat with Trapper and ferry the rest to another longer lake, drop it, fly back to get Trapper and what was left, and reload for the final flight home. That went well getting out of the small lake. I found a horse-shoe lake about 15 miles away that was perfect with longer stretches for takeoff. I landed and taxied to the upper part of the lower horseshoe.

I got out and started unloading. A gust of wind came up and took the little plane away from me in seconds and blew it backwards to the lower part of the horseshoe. So here I was across this lake from my plane, and now I had to hike all the way around the horseshoe to get to it. What a goat rope.

Finally, I got to the plane, taxied again across the pond, finished unloading, climbed back in and headed back to where Trapper and the rest of the meat was piled. I landed and found Trapper had made a pig of himself. I loaded everything up and made it out and back to the other lake, consolidated my load and continued my trip home to Soldotna. I decided after this escapade that I would not allow the allure of a herd of caribou with big racks to cloud my judgment when picking a place or pond to land. That postage-size pond was adequate for my Super Cub on most days, but one must think about what it would be like departing if the wind changed directions, or the load increased substantially after a successful hunt.

CHAPTER 6
ENATTY ENATTY

"Me Enatty, me scared." Those very words were scratched with what appeared to be a knife on the inside wall of a small, dilapidated cabin up Taylor Creek. Taylor Creek flows out of the Taylor Mountains in a westerly serpentine path, emptying into the lazy Holitna.

I had two hunters on the creek with me looking for a record bull moose, and it was an area where bulls hung out at this time of the season. Generally speaking, the big bulls would stay high on the hillsides fattening up in the willows, preparing for the rut. Often as I flew over these mountains, my eyes would catch the flash of antlers in the waning light as they browsed. But now it was pouring rain, and we were chilled to the bone. There were mobs of tiny vampires (Alaskan mosquitos) hungrily swarming around our heads.

Our small kicker motor grudgingly battled the swift current of the swollen stream. A shelter of any kind in such conditions would have been a welcome sight. Suddenly, perched on a bend near the meandering stream, the outline of a ghostly cabin appeared out of nowhere. There were no windows. The door hung open and cocked on several pieces of thin metal cut from a tin can. What was left of a handmade latch from a piece of weathered leather was chewed in half.

We immediately paused the hunting venture and carefully approached the opening. The loud rush of feathers from a great horned owl frightened from its perch filled the air. We fell back, startled, pulling our guns simultaneously to confront the potential danger. Realizing what it was, we breathed a sigh of relief and entered.

Though small, it afforded room for three to sit on a couple of handmade log stools and a five-gallon pail turned upside down. There was a small table in the middle of one wall while the back wall had a stove made from a metal can propped up with several river stones. There was a small diameter stovepipe sprawled on the floor with one end squeezed together with teeth marks that definitely looked bearish. Then we noticed the shaky writing on the other long wall. "Me Enatty, me scared."

Who was Enatty? I didn't know at the time, but later found out he was a native who lived remotely way up the Shotgun Creek, one of the three tributaries forming the Holitna.

One season later on I had several outfitted hunters in the Shotgun Hills hunting for caribou and moose. It was late in the season, and they had been very successful. All had gotten a nice bull caribou and appeared to have known what they were doing, since the meat was well cared for and salvaged properly. I had hauled all the meat out and given it away to townspeople in Red Devil, or so I thought. The trophy antlers I stashed for later transport to town and proper wrapping for shipment.

I started hauling the hunters and their gear out, and when I returned for the last fellow, he took me over to an alder patch and showed me a moose antler he had gotten from a bull he'd shot down on an east-running ridge roughly a quarter mile from the bottom.

I wasn't sure what he was thinking, though I had a pretty good idea, so I informed him that no way was that antler leaving the hill we were on without the meat (Alaska hunting regulations require all edible meat to be removed from the kill site before taking possession of the antlers), and he had to show me exactly where it was before I flew him back.

He said he fully intended to pack it up, but because everyone was ready to go and a storm was moving in, he didn't think he had time to do it. Current regulations that season and in that area called for either four brow tines on one side or 50 inches at widest spread. I gave the rack a glancing look and noted it did not qualify in the brow tine category, and the widest width looked close at best. I assumed he had measured it. He said he had marked the site of the meat with orange tape, which was good.

We took off and flew over and down that ridge, and sure enough, there it was lying helter-skelter here and there, indicating either he was a sloppy hunter or a wolverine or bear had already found the pile and claimed it. I headed back to Red Devil to coordinate with the other fellows for their flight back to Anchorage by charter flight.

Now I had a big job to do and was glad they were the last of my hunters for the season. At the top of the ridge where the moose parts were located, the hill flattened out nicely, offering a great place to land and take off from with a load, though not the most spacious site. I knew an arctic front was bearing down on us from Russia and probably would sprinkle the landscape with the season's first snow. It was cold enough so there was no problem with spoilage.

I stopped at my homestead to get a good night's rest and hit it early the next morning. When I awoke and looked out, my confidence in getting this done in a couple of days quickly eroded. It just wasn't going to happen. The snow kept falling. I had little doubt it was doing the same south in the Shotgun Hills.

Now I was concerned about finding the meat again. The antler still rested in that alder patch. At least the landing site was familiar, but the hill at the top of the ridge was now covered with fresh snow and what had looked okay for landing and taking off before would now begin to be a real challenge. If it kept snowing like it was, there was no way I would make it on tires. Those were the days of 26- to 29-inch bush tires. Now I sport 35-inch ones that could handle some pretty good snow but the arctic front dropped a couple more feet of snow, so there was no way on tires of any kind.

Finally the storm let up the third day, and after digging and stomping out a runway in the snow, I set sail for Port Alsworth to borrow some skis or wait for mine to be brought there from Soldotna. Another day passed, and they arrived. The problem was, there was no snow at Port Alsworth. The front had not dropped down that far, and they were still dry. That meant I had to carry my skis, a small bottle jack, some blocks and tools, and find a ridge near the site of the moose kill to land that was exposed and windblown clear of snow yet had snow patches nearby to take off from.

This could prove to be a real challenge. I began planning what I needed. I borrowed snowshoes and a sturdy backpack. The Shotgun Hills were between Port Alsworth and my homestead so it made no sense going so far out of the way to grab those items when I could borrow them and do the job on the way.

I set out with full tanks plus four extra cans of fuel. I knew it would be no small thing to come across a ridge with enough solid ground showing through to land with wheels and then change over to skis. But there it was. On my second loop of the area, about five miles away, I found what I was looking for and landed. In short order I had the small bottle jack out, positioned, and was jacking up one side. After removing the tire and wheel, I proceeded to install the Landis ski for that side, changed over, and did the same on the other side.

I was soon in the air circling the ridge looking for the moose meat. Though it was covered with snow, I knew about where it was heaped. I landed on top of the hill and did a figure eight, stopping back in my tracks closest to the ridge the meat was on. I had no illusions of hauling all of it off in one load. I figured at least three. The top of the hill was barely adequate lengthwise, depending on which way the wind was blowing. Now all I had to do was put on my snowshoes, shoulder my pack frame, and head out. Going downhill was easy, especially since I had no load.

But coming back up carrying a full pack frame was a challenge in the snow. I had no idea. Snowshoes are a nuisance without a load, but with a load in deeper powder snow, and uphill, they are a near impossibility. After many rest stops, I finally got to the top with the first load and decided after one more I would fly it over to the other rendezvous spot and take a breather while doing so. That plan worked well, at least before actually getting the plane in the air with the load.

After loading the pile of meat I had packed up so far in the plane, I crawled in, cranked up, and gave it full power. Nothing happened. The plane was stuck to the snow. No amount of coaxing changed the outcome. I worked the elevator control up and down. The skis were frozen to the snow. I had forgotten to wait a few moments after making the figure eight and then pulling forward, allowing the skis to cool. The friction running on the snow melts it, and when you stop suddenly, they freeze down. I needed someone outside the plane shoving the wing up and down as I applied full power. I guess I was the only candidate.

I applied full power, crawled out the plane door, walked out about halfway down the wing, and began shaking. It started to move. Now I had to get back inside pronto. I scrambled on top of the heel of the ski as the plane began accelerating toward the edge. I jumped in as it bolted over the edge and gained enough elevator control to fly it while my backside was still sticking out the door. I doubted I was the first aviator to do this stunt. I just didn't want it to be my last.

Having finally squirmed inside the cramped cockpit, I flew to the other hill and dropped my load. I dreaded the next loads, but at least on the last one I could head to Red Devil to give away the meat without having to unload and reload.

I headed off the hill and down over the Shotgun to follow it northerly, since it had begun snowing pretty hard. I was just above the treetops but out over the river when I passed a gravel bar. I made a mental note about it as a possible landing site if the weather worsened and I had to hang out somewhere for the night.

I hadn't gone very far, maybe ten miles, when another Cub zoomed out of the snow front going the opposite direction. It went over the top of me by what seemed inches and disappeared. That was it for me. I made a 180 degree turn and headed back to find that gravel bar. Finally there it was, and I quickly landed.

I unloaded the meat as it was so heavy, turned the plane around by hand, and tailed it into the bushes. I was getting my sleeping bag out of my seat cover, where I keep it to cushion the seat, when movement on the river caught my eye. I couldn't believe my eyes.

There was an old dugout canoe being poled across the river toward me. In it was a Native chap. I didn't realize it at the moment, but I was about to meet Enatty Enatty. Behind him on the opposite riverbank were several cabins and what looked like chained dogs, lots of them. They were making a ruckus.

I went down to the river to catch the canoe. Standing there was a slightly-built Native fellow, probably in his sixties. He didn't smile, mainly grunted a few unintelligible words, and motioned for me to get in. I asked if he would like the pile of meat. He seemed stunned and quickly nodded affirmatively. This would be like walking up to a person on the street of any city and handing them $1,000. This was life, meat for another hard winter.

When we arrived on the other side, I carried my pack and hung close behind him in the middle of the path as these mean-looking animals were leaping at the end of their chains to get at me. We went into his tiny cabin, hardly five-foot high max. One had to bend slightly to walk. The wood fireplace was going. Nearby was a radio, and it was on. Playing was Bush Radio with messages for those in the bush.

Enatty (his first name) Enatty (his surname) was waiting to hear if his brother had gotten to Sleetmute safely. Sure enough, the announcer came on and said Evan Enatty had arrived safely in town. After sitting a couple hours with few words spoken between us, I was motioned to go to the other cabin and sleep.

I grabbed my bag and started down the path paralleling the Holitna River. The almost-wild husky dogs were chained on each side of the pathway and leaped at me as I walked by just out of their reach.

The river flowed only a few feet away from the edge of the cabin. Being careful to stay in the middle of the path, I arrived at Evan's cabin. It was fairly tidy for what it was. The door was partly open, and in the doorway sat a cat. When I entered, I ducked as it, too, was quite low inside. I started a fire in the woodstove.

After spreading out my sleeping bag on Evan's cot, I lay down to sleep. Just above my nose on the low ceiling and on the wall to my left hung what appeared to be this man's entire life in a few photographs, a few mementos, and several useful tools. An old paring knife that had been sharpened so many times it looked like an ice pick was stuck in the wall.

After falling asleep, I was awakened by the cat pawing me, wanting to go outside and relieve itself. It was cold. I hurriedly got out of bed and opened the door, stoked up the fire again, and fell asleep. I awakened again but this time to the sound of scraping on the window. It was the cat wanting back in. I opened the door, and in ran the cat headed straight for my pillow.

The next morning, I had some coffee with Enatty, after which he poled me back across the Shotgun to my plane. I had often heard about these two brothers and how they would brag sometimes in town about smoking someone passing by on a raft. I thought if I ever ended up with one of those bad clients that you get occasionally and they wanted to drift the river, I could just drop them off a few bends above these two and wish them luck. (Just joking.)

Now I had some unfinished business to attend to. I had to fly back up on the mountain and finish moving the rest of that mountain of moose meat down to the gravel bar. This took a couple more trips, and then I stopped by that alder bush near the old camp and retrieved the marginal moose rack.

Now I was ready to head back to Port Alsworth. I topped off with fuel from the four spare cans, changed my skis back for wheels, put them inside the plane, tied the moose antler on the strut outside, and headed back.

Now I had to confront the last issue of this hunt, the marginal moose antler. It so happens that the resident game warden was a friend from way back—Ed Painter, who had a reputation for being hardnose, though fair. I heard tell he would probably turn in his grandmother if she broke the law. Prior to moving fulltime to this remote place, he lived in Soldotna as I did. In fact, we went to the same church there.

One time, while hunting on a drawn permit up in the Kenai Mountains for caribou and not having come across the herd, I was almost run over by a rutty bull moose and dropped it in its tracks. After dressing it out and packing the meat several miles one way, I found out that, of the two management units that came together right there, one had closed the day before and that moose very well could have been on the line or in that closed unit. I was staying in a forest service cabin, which I had not reserved.

About the time I got all the meat moved to the cabin, a plane showed up on the lake to drop a couple hunters off. They had reservations, and I was obliged to move out and set up camp in the rain in the middle of over a quarter ton of moose meat. It was not my idea of a very restful place to be in the midst of bear country. In fact, the two hunters who had arrived were there to hunt bears. They were the ones who advised me the unit had closed where I possibly had shot this bull.

Shortly thereafter, my charter plane returned on schedule to rescue me out of my dire straits. I was driving through town and saw Ed's truck and stopped him. He asked me what I had done. I couldn't believe he asked me that. I guess most people don't normally stop a game warden to just talk. I explained to him what might have happened. He retorted, "No, it's not a liner or marginal. If you shot it in American Pass, it had closed, and I have to come get it." Well, he did, and fast. He wouldn't even let me keep a little backstrap and for sure not the antlers. Now that was a lot of work for nothing. Well, since then, he always referred to me as "bandit," in a friendly sort of way.

So picture this. Here I am out in the boonies. His sweet wife, Kathy, had the only restaurant in Port Alsworth, and it was a good one. Not only was she an accomplished artist, she could cook up a plate of vittles like no one else. Well, I landed with this antler and pulled up outside the door of the restaurant just off the Alsworth runway. I got out and sauntered in to get a burger.

As I did so, I noticed out of the corner of my left eye that Ed was sitting in the corner at a table reading something, probably going over a bunch of tickets he had written.

I turned toward him and said hello with the best of intentions. He looked up and said, "Well how are you, you old bandit?"

When I came in, I was thinking to let him examine that antler with a measuring tape just to prove it out so there would be no problem shipping. Now I was thinking maybe I'd better get a burger and eat quickly, and hope he didn't get up and go out because if he did, he would see the antlers and for sure want to measure them.

Then I thought, maybe it would help if I offered to buy him a milkshake in his own restaurant. Kathy came over and said hello and asked for my order. I told her and said make it two, one for me and one for Ed.

So then he says, "What have you done now?"

I said, "Why nothing, just being neighborly." After that, we had a peaceful conversation while drinking our milkshakes. I was feeling hungry, so I decided to order a cheeseburger. I asked Ed if he would like one too.

He started squinting and looked me square in the eyes. "Are you sure you haven't done anything?"

I assured him I hadn't. After all that, I still felt a little hungry and asked Kathy what she had for dessert. Now this lady could do dessert like no other. And of course, I turned to Ed and asked him what he wanted for dessert, to which he abruptly replied, "Now I know you've done something. What is it?"

At that I confessed I had an antler tied on outside, whereupon I reached in my pocket and pulled out a tape measure and slid it across the table and asked him if he wouldn't mind going out there while I finished my dessert and measure it, and pretty please, while measuring, would he stand on it?

With that he almost turned the table over getting up, grabbing my tape, and stomping out the door. Meanwhile, I was trying to enjoy my dessert while sweating bullets. Even though I didn't shoot it and it was not a guided hunt but an outfitted one, this hunter still was under my watch, and though he may have messed up, it never bodes well for the guide or outfitter.

Ed was gone 15 minutes or so. Then the door squeaked open and in he came. He sat with this stern look on his face. He looked me square in the eyes and said, "If it had been an eighth of an inch smaller, I would have ticketed you."

Whew, those were the sweetest words I ever heard come out of that man's mouth. I thanked him, paid my bill, and headed home.

CHAPTER 7
THE WITCH LADY

Living and working on water of any kind—lake, river, stream, ocean—one always thinks about boats, from kayaks and canoes to power boats for fishing, hunting, or whatever. I had brought several boats from Soldotna to use, from 14- to 24-footers. Several I managed to tie on the floats of my Beaver and fly out, while larger ones I paid to have flown into Red Devil and ran them up the river to the homestead.

It so happened that a jon boat with no motor was owned by a friend of mine, Vince Spady, and his wife, Mary Lil, who taught school in Sleetmute. They had a homestead only ten miles upriver from mine, but with the twists and turns of the river, our actual properties ended up only about a mile or so apart.

Vince is an accomplished bush pilot with lots of experiences—most good but some not so good. In fact, I'm glad Vince is around because he provides me company in the stratospheric realm of Alaskan aircraft incidents.

Notice I said "incidents." Like the time I got a Sunday afternoon call from Roald Amundsen of MARC who said Vince had called in on a satellite phone and said he was stranded on the Skilak glacier somewhere with two elderly Christian ladies he had been showing the Kenai Peninsula sights to. He had called everyone he could think of to take some oil to him as an oil hose had broken and he had to set the plane down.

I was game to help them, so I jumped in my Super Cub and flew up toward the glacier looking for them. When I found them, they were waving and seemed excited that someone came to help. Vince had already marked out an area he thought I could land at between ice and boulders, and sure enough, I was able to get in and stop safely.

Now the hard part was about to take place. While I gave him the oil and we talked about taping the break in the oil line to get out of there, he asked me if I would take the little old ladies. Well, they weren't so little, and my Cub had only one seat behind me, but that didn't matter to them.

When I turned around to talk to them about flying them out safely, maybe one at a time, and maybe one would have to stay the night if Vince couldn't satisfactorily repair the oil hose, they had already crawled into my plane, one in the baggage and one in the seat. No way were they going to be denied getting out of there before dark.

I turned to Vince and suggested we work on the "runway" a little more so I could have an extra 50 to 100 feet to carry the extra weight. There were no obstacles, and as I remember, we even drained some gas from my tanks, leaving me enough to get to Sterling to drop them off at a small runway there and then fly on over to Soldotna.

It worked, and I made it off with them, leaving Vince to fend for himself. I heard later he ended up taking off, but his repair ruptured again, and he had to emergency land somewhere.

Anyway, Vince came to me one day and said he had a boat to sell, a real nice one about 18 feet, and he would take $500 for it as is, where is. Wow, it cost that much or double just to ship a boat like that out to our remote neck of the woods, so I jumped on it.

The usual disclaimer of "as is, where is" is jargon for when you buy it, you own it no matter what the condition. Well normally when I buy something like that from somebody, I never think about the "where is" part of the deal. Usually it is right in front of my eyes where I can examine it and make a judgment as to the "as is" and then drive off with it. But in this case, it was a whole lot different.

After I paid Vince, I asked him where it was so I could go get it.

He said, "At the Witch Lady's."

I said, "What did you just say?"

He said it again, at the Witch Lady's. She lived alone, way up-river near the Shotgun in a tiny cabin at a sharp double bend in the river. He said he thought her family was part of the Nogamute settlement that used to be on the east side of the river near some bluffs, but which had long since fallen into disrepair and all but disappeared. Also, he said he thought she might have some relation-ship to the Enatty brothers who lived further up the river.

I thanked him and began making plans to retrieve my boat.

I had heard from my friend Rocky McElveen that once he had a couple of moose hunters he was guiding, and he came around a sharp bend in the river on the upper Holitna and standing right in the river was a humongous bull moose. They paddled the raft to shore, got out, and prepared to fire away at the moose.

Just before they dropped the hammer on the bull, a shot rang out, then another, and the massive bull fell to its knees in the shallow water and rolled over dead. It was then they saw this old lady come out of the woods nearby holding an ancient rusty "point, bang, dead gun."

They rafted over to her and introduced themselves. They had just made acquaintance with the Witch Lady of the upper Holitna River. Her cabin was perched on a small rise off the river on the next bend. I needed to get in my C-185, fly to her cabin, look the river over real good, and land.

A few days later, it was my turn to make her acquaintance. I landed to the north, downriver. The water of the river is good, but it has a darker color due to vegetative material; hence, it is difficult to determine if there are obstacles lurking beneath the surface that could ruin your day. Rocks just under the surface give telltale signs, but a little deeper not so.

I landed without incident and taxied to her bank and jumped out, grabbed the front rope, and tied it off to a tree nearby. She was out of her tiny cabin and walked down the path with a .30-30 lever action Winchester in hand. I waved and waited. The sled dogs lining the path to her cabin were choking at their chain collars as they leaped in the air growling and barking. I was hoping she spoke English and not some dialect of the Athabascan Natives.

She gruffly asked what I wanted. I explained about the boat deal, and sure enough she nodded her head in a positive affirmation toward an old green boat off the path with weeds growing up and over it. Then she invited me in.

I was elated and eagerly followed her to the cabin. It was very low and built with "logs" that averaged two to three inches in diameter. There was hardly anything to it. It was better described as a stick palace with the emphasis on *stick*. I couldn't imagine a little old lady living like this alone in this unforgiving wilderness and surviving. She had her nets out and was catching a bunch of fish. She had drying racks filled. I am sure she used a lot of it for her dogs through the winter but subsisted on it herself as well.

I looked around at her meager existence and wanted to offer some help. I noticed her window facing the river was darkened with age and was nothing more than a piece of polypropylene. Temperatures in this country can easily go below minus 50 degrees Fahrenheit some winters.

Since I would be returning with a couple of fellows who would float the boat downriver, I asked her if I could bring anything for her. She got a piece of paper and pencil and began to write a list. It was long, including canning supplies, some food staples, and ended with a couple boxes of "thuty thuty" shells.

I asked if she had a tape measure so I could measure for a window and bring it back and install it for her. I departed letting her know I would be back within a week.

Several days later I returned with a couple friends who agreed to float the boat down to my homestead, hunting along the way, and I would meet them several days later there to take them back home. While they were flipping the boat and readying it, I went up to see her in the cabin and give her the things she ordered.

I will never forget what she said as she stepped out to greet me: "Who dem big guys?" I assured her they were with me, and all was okay. I went back and got the window I had made and installed it. It was nothing fancy, but fixed double pane was a huge improvement from what she had. At least now she could look out and see the river. Also, it had to be a bunch warmer come winter.

With the fellows in the boat and drifting downriver without a care in the world, I thanked her and left, never to return. I have often wondered since those days where she got her name and whether she still lived in that tiny cabin way upriver and out of touch with civilization.

CHAPTER 8

MY PLANE A TARGET

You just can't make this stuff up. What I am about to share with you is an event that happened while flying my DHC-2 Beaver remote to resupply my stock of fuel. I had taken along my faithful companion, Trapper. Often when I would stop at a fueling dock to refuel, he would slip over to my seat and sit patiently watching. He appeared to be the pilot. I had gotten him a silk scarf and goggles, which he wore with aplomb.

On this trip, however, he was sitting slightly behind me and between the pilot and passenger seats up front. Stacked behind him were at least four 55-gallon drums of aviation fuel. Tucked around them were several five-gallon cans of regular mogas (automotive gas) for outboard motors, snowmobiles, and four-wheelers. The right front seat was loaded with miscellaneous supplies, heavy canned goods, and the like.

It was a dangerous load. Outside, tied on the floats, I had several four-by-eight sheets of plywood cut in half longways. When carrying heavy loads like this, one has to observe the rear spreader bar to be sure it does not become submerged from too much weight. Not only can too much weight loaded aft affect the control of the plane in the air, it can adversely affect it on takeoff, especially heading downriver and stopping suddenly. I observed an aft overloaded Beaver one day at Lake Hood roll over backwards from such a condition.

On this day, the takeoff was long but uneventful. All three tanks in the belly were filled as were the tip tanks on the wings. The last thing I wanted to do was make any unscheduled stops.

Having departed Longmere Lake to the south, I pulled up the ten degrees of takeoff flaps I used, began a 30-degree bank turn to the right, and pointed my nose generally toward the outflow of the McArthur River into the Inlet. I was heading for a bench on the south end of Mount Spurr that led to a ravine that terminated at Chakachamna Lake. This led to the entrance into the infamous Merrill Pass, where the remains of numerous wrecked planes can be observed to this day. Some say over 29 wrecked planes can be counted there.

I had just passed 1,500 feet knowing I needed at least 3,500 feet to get through Merrill Pass, though 4,000 feet is my personal minimum. I was coming to Cook Inlet now, and I kept feeling nudges to my right elbow. It was Trapper wanting his usual attention, I thought.

But soon the nudges turned into more vigorous shoves as he tried to work his way from where he sat to my lap. That wasn't going to work. He began whimpering.

I started to resist, pushing back, until I sensed he was hurting. He became more insistent. That is when I noticed the wet floor and smelled gas a bit stronger than usual. Evidently one of the smaller cans had been overfilled, and with increasing altitude the fuel had expanded and some was being emitted. I realized his skin must be burning from sitting in this gas, so I glanced out of the window downward, took note of the Inlet that thankfully was fairly calm and near slack tide, and spiraled down to land.

Cook Inlet is not a place one wants to land floats if it is at all possible to avoid. Rip currents, waves, and tremendous tidal changes can and do make it an unfriendly and daunting place to land with floats. But I was over halfway across and decided under the circumstances to land.

By the time I was down, Trapper was in my lap. I quickly opened the door, and he, with my help, launched himself through the air without giving a thought for how high he was. He hit the water swimming, and he didn't look back. No amount of yelling got his attention. Though not numerous in Cook Inlet, I have observed killer whales while halibut fishing and was concerned. They have been known to rip huge moose to shreds and even giant brown bears trying to swim between the Alaskan Peninsula and Kodiak Island.

I became worried when I realized he was not going to return voluntarily. I quickly made room in the front passenger seat by shifting supplies around, cranked up, and started chasing him. As I approached, I decided the best course of action would be to straddle the swimming dog. I cut power when I got to him, using my forward momentum to overtake him but not so quickly that I would overshoot and he could get away at the rear. I was glad my load of two-by-eight plywood sheets were tied on the passenger side. I had to get down quickly on the front of the floats, or maybe even dangle on the crosswire between the floats, and somehow try to snag him with my hand.

Fortunately, with gentle coaxing, he came to my side of the floats where I grabbed and hauled him up in one fell swoop. He was rinsed off and not burning now and shook himself like an earthquake, thoroughly soaking me. I lifted him up into the plane while crawling in behind and pushing him to the passenger seat. No way was he going to the back of that plane again. I cranked up and we headed off on our route to Red Devil.

In years past, Red Devil, located on the Kuskokwim River in southwest Alaska and referred to as the white man's village, was the site of an old mercury mine that eventually played out and closed due to environmental reasons. It was situated about eight miles down-river from the Native village, Sleetmute. It being early October, the Alaskan PFD (Permanent Fund Dividends) had been mailed. I failed to put two and two together until the fireworks began.

As I approached the Kuskokwim, I noticed a fog bank overlaying the Red Devil area from Barometer Mountain. The fog extended downriver quite a ways and halfway upriver toward Sleetmute. I descended to get a better look and realized it would be best if I turned and went back to Sleetmute to land and wait it out. In fact, from there I could pretty much gauge if it was okay to try again.

The only problem was that as I flew low over the village and gravel runway to line up for a river landing, I noticed a couple of inebriated fellows with what appeared to be assault rifles waving and shooting in the air. I had no idea a couple of bullets had pierced my floats but quickly decided I wasn't going to stop there and wait out the fog. I turned and headed up the Holitna River to my homestead 35 miles away to land and wait an hour at least.

At 25 gallons an hour, the old R985 Pratt and Whitney engine had lightened my load by several hundred pounds, so it was a little easier to get airborne. Too, I took this time to unload the lumber and smaller cans of fuel and miscellaneous supplies. Now I was ready to return and attempt a landing at Red Devil and offload the barrels of fuel.

Sure enough, after skirting Barometer Mountain and overflying Red Devil, giving a wide berth to Sleetmute, I landed uneventfully, secured my plane and walked up to the hardware store.

Along the way I noticed a State Trooper's plane, a Cessna 206 parked on the ramp, and I was elated. I burst into the store to share what had happened. Everyone was sitting around the fireplace drinking coffee and spinning tales.

When I related what had happened earlier, one of the troopers spoke up and said, "Yeah, we know. Take a seat and have a cup of coffee. We were going in there, too, on a call out, and they shot at us. That's why we are here."

Evidently as soon as the money started flowing, some of the Natives from the village, which was dry at the time, beat it down to Red Devil to get booze and didn't waste any time satisfying their thirst. I won't go into the details, but one of the villagers had taken it out on his wife, who happened to be the daughter of a neighboring village's chief on the Stony River at Lime Village, with a chainsaw. The chief was on his way downstream to extract vengeance. That was the reason for the call to the troopers.

CHAPTER 9

SHOOT, DON'T SHOOT

"Ralph, is that you?" The VHF radio in my airplane crackled to life, startling me. This area of the Holitna is so far upriver and remote, one hardly ever hears another voice over the aircraft radio. I grabbed the mike and keyed it. "Yes, who is this?"

"This is Alaska Fish and Game, and we caught one of your guides on the river with clients shooting at swimming caribou." This is a definite no-no and explicitly warned against in the Alaska F & G Regs.

I answered, "Really, that's interesting since all my guides are up in the Shotgun Hills with clients. Besides, how do I know who you are for sure? You could be just a prankster or competitor."

"Well, he said his name was Tad and he works for you. We are going to report this when we get back to Bethel from our fish surveys."

I answered, "Well have at it." It can be disheartening to receive such a message, whether written or verbalized, since the state of Alaska maintains very tough and strict standards for professional guides.

As I flew along with my last client, ferrying him to a Shotgun Hills ridgetop to his spike camp for moose and caribou, my mind was racing, trying to imagine what happened back at or near our main camp on the Holitna.

I would just have to wait it out until I landed on the downriver gravel bar we used for ferrying our hunters from a river hunt to a mountain hunt in the hills. It was between the old town site of Nogamut and another called Kashegeluk, now pretty much returned to the land from which they came.

Hunting on the river that far up was usually very productive, but timing was critical with a cold snap sending the big bulls racing to and fro searching for a harem. Usually it brought them out of the hills where they have been hanging out, fattening up in the willows. The pre-rut phase causes them to go searching wherever to find cows, and one can hear them beating their huge antlers against the brush scraping off the velvet. Sometimes they will relieve themselves in huge puddles on the ground, marking the area. Grunting and challenging any other bulls, they crisscross huge tracts of land looking for available cows and eventually end up down at the river.

I dropped off the hunter at the spike camp and took off to check my other camps I had out. I hate working alone in such remote country with no help. At best, just one mistake and my airplane could easily end up in a heap of scrap metal, and at worst, I wouldn't be alive to tell the tale. So every landing and every take off had to be carefully calculated and accomplished, and this isn't easy when you are doing such work on gravel bars, ridgetops, and in all kinds of weather—especially wind—and loaded down, sometimes with external loads tied on such as huge moose and caribou antlers. Some days I would do as many as 30-plus takeoffs and landings, and many of these were new places I had never before landed.

Finally, I turned toward the gravel bar just below our main river camp. I arrived over the camp and buzzed it so Tad would know I was landing and get in the boat and come pick me up.

I was eager to hear what he had to say. Tad was a good fellow, a lifetime Alaskan, knowledgeable in the wilderness, and, on the world-famous Kenai River, a very successful professional guide. But this hunt was when he was younger, and most of us, if we are honest, would have to admit we didn't always use the best judgment in our younger years. Just exactly what happened, I couldn't imagine. This I knew: There were no other hunters under contract by me in that camp.

As I touched down and pulled over to the tiedown I had made in the gravel to hold my plane if the winds came up, I could make out Tad in our boat racing down the river to get me. After tying the plane securely, I walked to the edge of the river just as he arrived. He jumped out and asked me if I wanted to drive back and I said I would.

I kept waiting for him to say something about the radio contact. He made no mention. He was jovial to the point of frustration for me. We pushed out and headed back upriver to our camp. We made small talk along the way and still no mention of the incident. Finally we arrived back at camp and pulled the boat up and secured it. As we made some dinner, I couldn't wait any longer. I asked, "Tad, do you have anything to say about anything important today?"

He looked at me kind of dumbfounded and said, "No, not really, what do you mean?"

"I mean about the caribou swimming the river, and you had a couple of fellows and Alaska Fish and Game happened to come around the bend heading up to Shotgun Creek to do salmon surveys, and they got you on video and heard you telling those fellows to shoot."

Tad's response was quick and to the point. "Oh that, well I was sitting in camp here and a couple of lost hunters came off those hills above us and asked me if I would run them upriver to their camp since their friend didn't know they were lost and had ended up downriver quite a ways. As a good Samaritan, I told them I would and loaded them in the boat and headed upriver. About that time, a whole herd of caribou started swimming across the river. Some were big racks and they grabbed their guns and started shooting. I hollered at them and said, 'Don't shoot,' and then about that time Fish and Game showed up and stopped us and wanted our names for doing it. They said they heard me say 'Shoot,' but I told them I said 'Don't shoot.'"

At this point, I broke into the explanation and told Tad that they were going to report it, that they had a video, and they claimed he said shoot. "So which was it Tad? Shoot or don't shoot?"

Tad answered me, and I believe truthfully, "Don't shoot."

So that is the story I went with.

The season ended, and I heard nothing. Christmas came and went and still nothing. Then in March of the next year, I got a call from the game warden in the area, Scotty Gibbons. We had known each other for a long time.

There was a time I would take my boat dealers from the west coast on hunts, but didn't charge them. It was mostly PR stuff. Scotty became aware of me in the area and wanted to know what I was doing since it appeared to him I was acting as a guide. Well in a way I was, but I wasn't charging. It was a gray area, and he encouraged me to jump through the hoops and get my guide license. I really didn't want to go that far with it, but I complied. It was extensive and tough, but I finally made the grade and obtained my Alaska Registered Guide-Outfitter license. It was then that I decided to branch out and really operate as a guide, especially after I left the boat business in California.

Now here we were again, looking each other in the eye and doing so in my living room at my home in Soldotna, only this time it had to do with the "shoot, don't shoot" incident. Scotty reminded me that a licensed guide has 30 days to report a known violation. It had been almost six months, and I had not reported it.

I simply asked Scotty how he knew about it. He told me that a couple of Fish and Game biologists had turned it in.

I then asked him why I should have been required to do so too. He told me it was a requirement. I didn't want to argue with him about it, and neither did I want to hire an attorney and fight it out in court, but the fact of the matter was that even if it had happened, it was hearsay as far as I knew.

I didn't observe it. I received a call on my radio's 122.50 frequency that I monitor from an unknown person who said they were Fish and Game, saying what they had heard and seen, and that they were turning it in. From my point of view, I saw no requirement to report it since it was Fish and Game themselves. Besides, I didn't have any firsthand knowledge of the incident. Case closed. Ultimately, Scotty agreed.

CHAPTER 10

FORGOT GEORGE

I have messed up a few times in all my years of flying hunters and fishermen around and setting up camps. Most have been minor mistakes, though they seemed major at the time to those on the ground.

I learned early on to never pack food in black garbage bags. For starters, it attracts heat, which is not conducive to preservation of food supplies. But the main reason is explained by how easy it is to make a mistake and grab a black garbage bag thinking it is garbage and haul it out a few days later, when in reality you just brought it in loaded with important food supplies. It doesn't take long for a camp full of hungry guys to sorely miss it, and they aren't inclined to be forgiving, because when you find it out, you still are a day or so from getting it back to them. (Though it probably was

thrown away and you have to try to figure out what they need and are missing by that time.)

But to lose track of a camp of guys when you are the only one who knows about them, especially their whereabouts, can be disastrous. Most would have families who would be calling in due course of time, but there are some who go out and are loners and not in contact with anyone in particular about their plans. I have heard about this happening. It's not often, but it does happen.

I had my own lapse of memory one time with George. Knowing how much he loved fishing, I could bait him like I would a fish, offering a chance to fish for helping me build something. George loved to build, but I think he loved fishing most of all.

I needed an actual dock to pull up to on the Holitna River that I could tie my plane to, keeping the wingtip off the bank of the river a ways, and a place to moor a fishing boat. It was tricky because you had to build it in such a way that you could winch it up out of the river in the fall for winter freeze-up. The freeze-up generally didn't break the dock. It's the spring thaw that does it when huge chunks of ice crash swiftly into anything in their path and sweep it downriver.

I asked George one day if he would like me to fly him remote to a fishing hole where he could fish almost nonstop, not only out in front of the camp but be able to get in a boat and go up or downriver and fish any number of species of fish to his heart's content. George was all in.

We loaded up the C-185 with extra fuel for boat gas, some food stuff for a week or so, and headed out to the Holitna homestead. Of course George had his normal array of fishing tackle. We landed and got settled in. I showed him what I wanted as far as the dock, and as he always does, he gave his very good input. Basically you just gave George an idea of what you wanted, maybe a sketch on a napkin, and he would do the rest, and you would usually like it. He truly was gifted.

After getting the job outlined, we jumped in the boat with our fishing gear, and we headed downriver, around the first bend and up to the head of the next bend where the heavier current indicated a deep hole. We anchored at the top of the hole and began casting.

It was a cloudy day, which was perfect for fishing Sheefish. Sheefish are in the whitefish family and live up to their reputation as the freshwater tarpon of the north. These fish only exist in certain rivers, and the Holitna is one of them. Though they can reach weights over 50 pounds, on the Holitna a big one would run around 35 pounds.

As the small fry go downstream after being hatched upriver, these hefty fish lurk deep in the holes, which their sun-sensitive eyes prefer, waiting for the fry to pass overhead. The fishing is extraordinary on cloudy days. It is not uncommon to have them leaping out of the water a foot or two in pursuit of these fry. I have literally sat in my boat and gotten wet so many were breaking water nearby.

Needless to say, George was enthralled. It was love at first sight. He fished his heart out and didn't want to stop. Finally, we headed back to the homestead, and he thanked me for the opportunity. He assured me he would get to work on the dock soon and get it done. The next day, I loaded my things in the C-185 and cranked up to leave. I had told George I would be back within a week or so.

By the time I was in the air, the boat was gone. As I flew a semi-circle around the homestead, I came over that sheefish hole, and sure enough, there was George already anchored up and fishing. He just couldn't get enough of it.

I flew off toward the Chigmit Mountain Range to the east and home to Soldotna. I busied myself around the house with work I had going on until a call came from my office in California. I needed to fly down to Sacramento on some urgent business. I fueled my P210 and headed out flying across the Gulf of Alaska and on down to California.

A week had already gone by in Alaska, and then in California, because I was so busy and had so many things to do, a couple weeks flew by there. I had completely spaced it that George was out on the Holitna. In those days, hardly anyone ever passed by the homestead on the river until hunting season, which began September 1. That was still over a month away.

One day something came up that jogged my memory about poor George, and I panicked. I tried to remember exactly when I dropped him off. Was it three weeks ago now or could it be a month?

I immediately packed my stuff and headed to the airport to fly back up. That trip usually took one day (nine to ten hours of actual flying), depending on weather of course. I arrived in Soldotna and went shopping for supplies. I was thinking, for what? When I got there, George, if he were still surviving, would be ready to come home never to go back. But I don't go anywhere without carrying something like fuel or supplies of some kind. I loaded up with extra fuel, more supplies, and took off. It is about a two-hour flight.

As I approached the homestead, I began letting down. I could see the bend in the river where the sheefish hole was. As I got closer,

I thought, oh my goodness, the boat is still there. Did George just pass away in this fishing heaven? Was I going to look down and see a skeleton?

I was nervous as I pulled power more and dropped lower. Now I was just above the treetops and coming fast for the boat. As I passed overhead and looked down, I saw this shaggy, unshaven creature stand wobbly to its feet and lift an arm. I couldn't tell if he was so mad he was flipping me off or just waving to me because he was glad I finally came back. I wasn't sure.

I lined up to land and taxied up to a brand-new dock. What a beautiful sight. George had outdone himself. He even had a slip on the inside of the dock for a boat with tie downs. As I exited the plane, I could see a boat coming full speed from downriver. It was George for sure.

My mind began to race. I remembered those stories he told about some of his actions before God saved him, like the time in Homer when three mean guys accosted him in a bar and he invited them outside, whereupon he laid them out with a two-by-four and the Homer cops ran him down going out of town. George was sure he was going to be arrested, but they thanked him because those three bad guys gave them a lot of problems and the cops didn't know how to handle them. They did however suggest he never come back to Homer.

Or the time he was going down Lake Clark on his snow machine and ran into a Native fellow whose snowmobile had quit running. He was cold and desperate. George readily offered to pull the man to his house, which he did. Later that night—after a bit too much hooch for all of them—the brother of the fellow he rescued came out of the bedroom and looked across the room. "Is that a white guy over there?" asked the brother. He then proceeded to go back in the bedroom, grab a .30-30, and come back into the living area. He pulled the lever down to put a live shell into the chamber to shoot George. That's as far as he got with his ill intentions.

George was no one you wanted to meet in a dark alley in those days, and in short order that Native fellow paid for his ill-advised attempt to put an end to George. He didn't give any real details of what happened after that, but for sure the gun was broken in two pieces. Whether it was over his head or the nearest wall, it doesn't matter. George abruptly ended his social visit, ran outside, hopped on his snow machine, and got out of Dodge.

Now it was my turn. I heard the motor get close and felt the dock rock as the boat slammed into it. Oh no. He was really mad. I had my trusty "bear spray" on my hip loaded with 350-grain mega bear bullets. I placed my right hand on it as I turned to confront George. In my heart I was praying for a peaceful resolution to my obvious negligence.

As I turned and our eyes locked, I saw that twinkle in his eye that only God and fishing can bring, and I began to relax.

It was then that good ol' George said these words, "Brother, why in the world did you come back so soon?"

CHAPTER 11

GEORGE ATE
THE EVIDENCE

I met George in 1992 through a mutual acquaintance. First and foremost, he was a fisherman. Second, his carpentry skills were legendary. Lastly, though addictions ruled his life early on, George came to a saving knowledge of Jesus Christ that so dramatically transformed his life he traded in his addictions for a walk with the Lord. This transformation evidenced itself by his becoming a fisher of men, a carpenter for the Lord, and a freed man from the slavery of addiction.

It was this transformed George that I knew well and ultimately introduced to Franklin Graham, who in 1995, upon hiring George for some personal carpentry work around his cabin in Alaska, realized what a unique and talented individual he was and brought him onboard with Samaritan's Purse, a world-wide relief organization for which he served faithfully until God called him home in the spring of 2016. We would never question God's timetable, but everyone who knew and worked with George would readily admit that he left some big shoes to fill, and heavy hearts.

I attended his funeral and burial out at Port Alsworth. His

carpenter boys nailed together a fine-looking coffin of wood. A handmade cross was nailed to the top of it. Flowers were placed there too.

At the head of the box was the word *tetelestai*. This is the Greek verb in the past perfect tense meaning "to finish or end." It is the same word used by Jesus as recorded by the Apostle John in verse 19:30 as he hung on the cross for the sins of every person, crying out, "It is finished."

George's work on earth was finished, perfected. He served faithfully until the end.

His wife, Debbie, clung tightly to the end of his coffin, tears streaming down her cheeks. Slowly they let the coffin down into the hole. His boys then came with a plastic container and gently let it down on top. I thought maybe it was a bunch of old fishing tackle and hip boots, but no, it was Buddy, his faithful dog who went everywhere with George.

George once remarked to Debbie, "If Buddy dies before I do, just shoot me." Buddy passed, then George shortly thereafter. She told me later that in the hospital on his deathbed as he looked up toward heaven with his last breath he cried, "My God, my glorious God."

We miss you, George, and we thank you for the memories you left. On several occasions I have heard Franklin declare, "I miss George."

On Memorial Day weekend, over 25 years ago, George suggested a trip to Eshamy Bay over on the east side of the Kenai Peninsula that borders Prince William Sound. We flew my C-185 and landed in Eshamy Lake, the headwaters of a small creek that spilled into the bay about a half mile away. George assured us it would be loaded at that time of the year with cutthroat trout, and the limit was ten each. There were three of us, and we were all in.

We landed and taxied up to the east end of the lake and tied down near an old tent platform where the lake flowed out and down to the bay. We merely spread out our sleeping bags on the platform with the stars of heaven as our ceiling. But first we hiked down the creek to check out our surroundings.

Along the way we passed an Alaska Fish and Game shanty that looked like a first-class outhouse sitting by the stream. There were tubes and such crisscrossing the tiny stream for whatever reason. On the shanty was hanging a clipboard with pen and paper attached for writing notes. The observation for May 30 was, "We caught a Dolly Varden with a Hooligan attached to its anus."

We kept walking and broke out down the hill overlooking beautiful Eshamy Bay and a high-six-figure log cabin with a heliport provided for the "hard"-working biologists of Alaska F & G. Several of them were spread out around the bay with fishing poles in hand doing what any honest sports freak would do: fishing. What they were fishing for—and by the appearance of bent-over fishing poles, catching—we had no idea. We could only surmise. Cutthroat trout? We decided we wouldn't be welcome there, so we turned and headed back uphill to our fishing hole.

What a fishing hole it was! In short order, we limited out and had 30 nice cutthroat trout loaded in the float compartments, minus several we cooked over our fire and ate for dinner that night. We were kicking ourselves that we hadn't thought to bring some fresh lemons. We soon turned in for one of the most peaceful nights I have ever experienced sleeping under the stars.

Early the next morning I awoke from my stupor, rolled out of my sleeping bag, and made my way to the nearest fishing pole. In short order I had one on and landed. There was a small puddle of water behind me. I laid the fish in and cast again. *Bam*, another strike, and my fishing pole bent downward and danced a jig.

This was fun, until . . . suddenly, out of nowhere, I felt a tap on my shoulder. I just about leaped right out of my own skin while reaching for my .44 magnum revolver. There stood a squirrely, skinny, wimpy, odd sort of fellow. He quickly announced he was Alaska Fish and Game and that the area was closed and off limits because the run of cutthroat trout was down to a minimal 195 counted.

My mind's calculator didn't waste a moment coming up with the conclusion, unknown to him, that the real number was more like 165, less two more—one in the puddle behind me and one on the line, which I landed in front of him. I kept that secret of course but asked him why the regulations showed it was open and the limit was ten each, and by the way, how do I know you are Fish and Game?

He immediately ripped open his jacket revealing a shallow bust covered with an old, faded Alaska Fish and Game tee shirt that had seen better days and could better be used as a rag.

I said, "Really, that is your proof? Why, I have several tee shirts like that I bought at the store, and they are a whole lot newer and more becoming than what you are wearing. So if I were wearing one of those shirts, I would be Fish and Game too?"

He didn't answer. He simply asked for my name, phone number, and address. He informed me it was a special closure, and it was my duty as a responsible citizen to check in with the department before going fishing to see that nothing had changed in the regulations.

I suggested that if that were true, it was his duty—if he and the department were so concerned with the low number of the run—to make up a special closure sign and place it up there to inform folks like us, but I understood that might take him away from his fishing fun down on the bay. The fact was, we would have honored it. In the end, I refused to provide my name and address, whereupon he turned to go and reached down to take my two fish.

I stopped him, suggesting it would be in his best interest of good health to just head back down the path to his fancy log cabin and go back to fishing his hole and catching his own fish. He said he wanted it as evidence. I said as far as I was concerned, he was from another planet and had no authority over me or the natural resources.

He left in a huff. The fellows were awake by this time, of course, dressed and ready to fish. We caught a few more, but the heart of our fun had been stabbed to death, so we packed up shortly and departed.

As we flew back, we talked about how my airplane tail number was like waving a flag with my address on it, and as ticked as he seemed to be when he departed, if he were legit, he probably had a radio phone of some kind and had already called it in and reported it. If that were true, we might have the troopers waiting down at Longmere Lake where I park the plane on my lot. That's when George suggested we have a huge trout fish fry along the shores of Skilak Lake, and besides, it was past lunchtime.

After that fry, I was so stuffed I couldn't stomach another trout for years. Shortly thereafter, we landed and guess what, not a person was in sight.

Later, in the early fall, I got a call from the troopers in Soldotna. They said they wanted to come over and see me and asked when I would be available. I asked what it concerned, since by this time the Eshamy Lake fiasco had been completely forgotten. That was what it was about, so I said it would take several weeks to finish out the hunting season and to call again in a month.

Sure enough, right on schedule, Officer Chuck Rogers called, whom I knew, and showed up at my door. He was warm, friendly, and we did some chit chat for a while before getting down to the business at hand. He asked me about how many we caught, and I said exactly the limit the first day and the second day just a few and we left.

He said he looked up the regulations and didn't understand what the problem was since the regulations definitely said ten each and there was no complaint that we had gone over the limit. He said the main thing was the insubordination. I must have frightened the fellow.

I explained to Chuck about the special closure, the lack of a sign to inform anyone, and the fact that they found plenty of time to fish themselves. I suggested that if he had been in my place under the same circumstances, he probably would have had a similar reaction. I think he agreed.

He nodded, made a couple notes, thanked me, and left. That was it.

CHAPTER 12

CHAIN ON MY PROPELLER

I happened to stop by the Soldotna airport one day to check on my airplanes and ran into Roald Amundsen, founder of MARC. Having been a missionary in Nome for some 20 years, he felt a call to set up an aviation-oriented ministry in Soldotna to serve the many churches and mission groups scattered throughout Alaska. The ministry was the kind one would feel comfortable donating to simply because Roald and his wife, Harriet, lived simple lives, serving and honoring God in all they did.

Roald had some bills to pay and an airplane to sell to do it, and he asked me if I would be interested in it. I inquired as to what plane it was, and it turned out to be one of the original 336 Skymasters that Cessna built in those years. It was fixed gear and had inline twin engines—one in front pulling like a normal single engine and one in the rear pushing. It was affectionately referred to as a Mixmaster push/pull. I knew it hauled a pretty good load and decided it might serve me well making runs out to Red Devil; plus they could use the money to pay some bills. I had never flown one, and I was assured a check pilot would be furnished for me. For the first time, someone stood by their word.

After a thorough check ride by Dave Cochrane, who at the time was one of the mission's main pilots and mechanics, I felt ready to tackle anything. I loaded it up and made a couple runs to Red Devil and felt pretty good about it.

Then one day, I got the crazy idea to fly it across the Gulf of Alaska and down to Sacramento. That turned out to be a flight to remember. My wife and I loaded up and pulled up to the MARC fuel pumps to fuel. When I tried to start the plane and depart, the front engine coughed and backfired causing a fire. The folks there were on top of it quickly, and we got it put out. They checked it over and all seemed to be well other than a couple of wires slightly singed. I should have taken it as a bad omen and canned the trip, but no, I had planned it and I was going.

We took off to the east toward the Kenai Mountains and climbed high enough to clear them and leveled out. All was going well as the Gulf of Alaska appeared in our windshield as we crossed the mountain range. Suddenly, the front engine just quit. My wife didn't seem to be too disturbed by it and kept reading. After all, we had two engines. But to cross the Gulf of Alaska with one engine already down wasn't exactly my cup of tea, so I made a casual 180 back toward Soldotna.

I was a bit reluctant to try to restart the front engine after what had happened on the ground prior to take off but decided to anyway. Wow, it started right up. So I did another 180 and headed out to sea. We were coming up on Montague Island when it quit again. By this time I was concerned enough to turn toward Valdez and make a precautionary landing.

After killing off a dozen or so seagulls on landing, I taxied up to an FBO and inquired about a mechanic. The mechanic on hand happened to be a fellow from Soldotna who had moved there and had some knowledge about this plane. He checked it out, got it running again, and then advised us to just take off and point it to Anchorage and take a commercial flight south.

I took his advice. The plane ran okay again for part of the way, then the same engine conked out, and we flew it into Anchorage International on one engine and parked it at the air taxi shack. We checked on a reservation south, got a close connection, tied the plane down where it was, and departed. We didn't have time for any formalities. The trip south was to be a quickie, and I figured I would just pick it up on the way back through, fly it to Soldotna, and get it serviced.

That was all fine and dandy except when I came back through, I forgot it and went on commercially to Soldotna.

Weeks went by.

One day I ran into Dave Cochrane out at the Soldotna airport, and he asked me if I had sold that Skymaster I had bought from them. I scratched my head trying to remember what he was talking about, and it suddenly dawned on me about that airplane. I had completely spaced it. Where in the world was that plane?

He informed me it was at the air taxi shack in Anchorage and had several rolls of orange tape all over it with some kind of signs attached. Also, he said there was a huge heavy-duty chain on the front prop with a padlock. I was astounded. I had been so busy and preoccupied with some other matters, I had completely forgotten about this plane.

Late afternoon the next day I bought a one-way ticket on Southcentral Airline to Anchorage to get the plane and face the music. When I got there, it wasn't a pretty sight. The right tire was flat. I opened the door and put the key in and turned on the master and the two-way radio would only receive. The battery was so low it wouldn't turn the rear engine over.

I called the ground personnel and announced I was there to

get the plane, and they rushed right over. They appeared quite up-set and demanded $2,700 in tie-down fees. I pulled out my wallet and tried to hand them a Visa and they refused it. They demanded cash. I didn't have that kind of cash on me and told them so. They suggested I fly back and get it and call them again when I arrived. Then they left.

I was upset about their attitudes and wondered how much of that money would go to the airport authorities. I decided not to waste my ticket there, much less have to buy two more to return and come back, so I walked over to the Sea Air hangar and talked to an evening mechanic on duty. He was kind enough to lend me an air tank and said at his break he would come over with a jump to get the rear engine going. I figured the front engine wouldn't run anyway, and if they were going to chain an engine to help me, they chained the right engine.

About 10:00 p.m. the mechanic showed up and helped me get the airplane jumped. I started the rear engine. It ran fine. I had enough fuel to safely get to Soldotna.

I turned on the master avionics switch and hoped the partially charged battery would help it to work. No luck. I couldn't remember the light signals for communication with the Tower in circumstances like these, so I set the brake, got out, and went into the air taxi shack and looked up the tower number and called them. They answered, and I told them my situation down at the taxi shack whereupon they informed me about the blinking green and the steady green, etc. They said they would be looking for me starting to taxi and talk me through it.

It was after 11:00 p.m. when I got my light signal clearance and began taxiing out to Runway 6 Left. I took the greater portion of the runway and was glad I did. That front propeller was a terrific drag as I took off and finally cleared ground and turned south to-ward Soldotna in the dark. I crossed Turnagain Arm and got a little uneasy when that engine began to surge some. I almost turned back and bagged that crazy venture but pressed on.

I landed at Soldotna airport uneventfully just before midnight. I parked the plane right in front of the MARC hangar door, got in my car, and headed home.

By 7:00 a.m., my phone was ringing off the hook. It was the folks at MARC wondering what in the world had happened. They couldn't believe I flew this airplane out of Anchorage International with one engine chained and that orange tape plastered all over it.

I got dressed and went down and explained.

It was not long after that I put the airplane up for sale as is, where is. I can't remember what they found was the problem with the front engine, but it was fuel related and they fixed it. I even made some money on the sale, but after that experience, there was no way I would own another plane like that, much less try to fly it across the treacherous Gulf of Alaska.

I had the plane registered to my business Holitna Wilderness Adventures out on the banks of the Holitna River. I don't get mail there, so I never heard again from those fellows in Anchorage. I suppose after they failed to get the cash, which I fully suspect would have gone into their own pockets, they dropped it.

CHAPTER 13

CHEAPER BY THE DOZEN

During my years transitioning between California and Alaska, I would fly back and forth between the two states, sometimes monthly in both winter and summer. All of my flying experience during this time was in reciprocating aircraft with tricycle gear, both single and twin engine. I had flown in bush airplanes called taildraggers quite a bit with friends in Alaska but had never owned or flown one.

There is a marked difference when landing and taking off in these two different gear configurations. On the one hand, the tricycle configuration consists of a nose wheel up front and a pair of main landing wheels positioned at or near the main doors of the aircraft where the pilot enters and exits. This design is very forgiving when taking off and landing. It is primarily used on normal, hard-surfaced airports. They can work very well on improved grass runways too. I have also observed them with a heavy-duty nose gear and oversized nose wheel landing on some smooth ridges and even tidal beaches. Folks like the Wilder family (father Dave and his son

Lyle), who own Lake and Peninsula Air, and others, do it with precision and ease in 206s.

On the other hand, the tail dragger consists of a tail wheel located in the extreme rear under the tail feathers, with the main landing wheels at or near the front door of the aircraft but further forward. This design is best for landing in remote, unimproved landing sites but is less forgiving when landing and taking off, especially in crosswinds. It has a pendulum effect, and if one is not careful—especially in crosswinds—it can get away from the pilot and easily ground loop, spinning the plane around and causing major damage to the wing on the side it is turning toward.

It can be operated on or off airports but with a clear advantage doing off-airport landings. It is ideal to land in softer material and is easily modified for ski and float operations. That is not to say a tricycle gear cannot be adapted to do the same. I mention all this to explain that if I intended to earn my wings as an Alaskan bush pilot, I would have to own and operate a tail dragger and fly it enough to build the necessary experience to safely operate and make accurate judgments when hauling loads in and out of short landing areas, with or without obstacles, and with various kinds of ground conditions—soft, bumpy, high weeds, wet or dry.

On one of my visits back to Sacramento, I noticed a hangar with the name Union Flights at the executive airport where I based my plane. Parked around it were numerous PA18 Piper Super Cubs, the bush plane of choice of Alaskan bush pilots. One trip I counted a couple dozen. They were all painted white with red-and-blue trim. They had no Alaskan options, just tiny tires and wheels with skirted landing gear and standard propellers.

I left one of my business cards stuck in the door of one of the planes with the message handwritten on it: "I have an interest in buying one of these Super Cubs. How could anyone make use of so many bush planes in the middle of California?" Unbeknownst to me, there was a big need to patrol gas pipelines for major utilities in California, such as PG&E.

This went on for about a year in the early 80s. I'd leave cards and hoped someday they would have a worn-out one they would want to sell cheap.

I never heard a word from them until one day out of nowhere I got a call from the son of the owner of Union Flights, and he asked me if I still had an interest.

I tried to keep my enthusiasm from bubbling over and being too obvious. I assured him I still had an interest.

Then he dropped a bombshell. He asked if I would be interested in half of his fleet, explaining that they had lost a major portion of their contract with PG&E and had to sell a bunch of airplanes quick.

Whoa! Had I just heard correctly? My heart skipped a beat as my mind processed what he'd said. I told him I would be right out and we would discuss. I had been exposed to these planes in Alaska enough to know full well the market potential, and, being in marketing, I was all in if the price was right considering age, total time on airframe, and time since major overhaul on engine and equipment. Whether they had been wrecked or not wasn't much of a factor in Alaska, as there was hardly a Cub to be found there that had not been broken at least once.

As I raced out to the airport to meet with him, I still had not given a thought as to how I might get them all to Alaska, the risk involved, or the cost. For myself, I had never owned, much less piloted, a single taildragger.

Regardless, when I arrived and introduced myself and we began our tour of the planes in their fleet that they wanted to sell, what I found was a treasure trove of bush aircraft begging to go to work in Alaska, America's last great frontier. Of the number they wanted to part with, some had very high-time airframes and engines, some had mid-time, and, to entice me, they even threw in a couple low timers for good measure. There was even an agriculture model that was built in 1959. It had a swayback fuselage.

The newest model had my name all over it and was a 1976 with low numbers. Their shop was clean and neat, and they showed me how meticulously they maintained their whole fleet. Several had been rebuilt multiple times because of the high-time airframes. One had an engine that had gone to TBO (time before overhaul) twice and was working on its third engine overhaul. That particular aircraft had 22,000+ hours TT (total time) on the air frame. Many had 12,000 to 15,000 hours TT on the air frames. They all had current annuals and were airworthy. They all had a simple radio package consisting of one 360-channel VHF, as well as basic VFR instruments, standard propellers, tires, wheels, and brakes.

At that time in Alaska, a Piper bush plane usually carried modifications like extended baggage, oversize bush wheels and tires, three-inch extended gear, and a Borer prop that was longer (one of the reasons for  extended gear) with flatter pitch, making for faster takeoffs and climbs (which is most important in bush flying due to short landing sites and heavy loads). With average time on engine and airframe one would sell for mid $30,000. Very few of Union Flight's planes had any history of being bent, but in Alaska that didn't particularly carry a lot of resale value for the normal Alaskan buyer.

So what did they want for all these airplanes? That they wanted to sell as one lump sum was no secret. That they would take a lesser price to make such a deal also was no secret. The final negotiation was inked with the stipulation they would provide me with a check ride and a place to keep them for at least a couple months as I made arrangements to fly them north one at a time.

With that, we shook hands, did the paperwork, and I was the proud owner of a bunch of Piper Super Cubs that I didn't know how to fly.

CHAPTER 14

THE TRENCH (A TRIP TO REMEMBER)

I excitedly began to plan my first flight to Alaska in a bush aircraft. One thing was certain: All of these trips would be navigated over terra firma and would exclude the more dangerous Inside Passage route, which consisted mostly of water and very few fueling stops. I inquired of other pilots who had made the trip, and after pouring over sectional maps, I had a pretty good idea of what my route would be.

One section of the trip made a special impression on me. It was an area above Prince George, British Columbia. From there, if one took a heading of approximately 310 degrees and held that heading for many hours and hundreds of miles, he would arrive at the famous Alcan Highway just east of Watson Lake, passing through a veritable trench between the far northern end of the Rocky Mountain Range to the east and the Cassiar Mountain Range to the west. The Rocky Mountain Trench, as it's called, begins just out of a town called McKenzie. It proceeds over Williston Lake, one of the longest lakes I have ever overflown, then transitions to a river that dribbles out onto a tundra plain through which the Alcan Highway snakes a path.

I was pumped. Armed with my aviation sectional maps marked up with my route, locked and loaded with my survival rifle, and packed with survival food, cooking gear, a small tent, sleeping bag, and air mattress, etc., I headed for the airport to depart.

Supposedly a check pilot would meet me to give a check ride. I waited around for about an hour, and when he didn't show, I decided to pack my gear and get on my way, albeit tentatively. I had heard so many stories of ground loops, admittedly I was apprehensive.

On the positive side, it was a beautiful day in May and the weather up the West Coast was ceiling, altitude, visibility unlimited (CAVU). Of all the planes to choose from for my maiden flight, I chose the oldest with the most hours since this was an experimental flight for me. I figured that if I ground looped, I wanted it to be in the oldest, least valuable plane.

On the negative side, with the high time hours on it, if there were going to be problems in my learning curve, this was the plane that would provide the excitement. Not only did it have over 22,000 hours on the airframe, the engine was pushing 1,900 TT SMOH (since major overhaul), and it was on its third overhaul. With a 2,000 hour TBO (time to be overhauled, as recommended by the engine manufacturer), well, that's considered high time. I asked a dear friend of mine, B Alsworth, a gifted, genius mechanic, what he thought. He said, "Keep flying it. It must be a good engine. I've had brand new engines blow up." I followed his advice until my dear mother heard about it and gifted me with a newly overhauled engine. To this day, I am still flying that plane and engine.

All of the higher performance reciprocating aircraft I was accustomed to had fuel injection. The *O* in the model designation of this engine stood for carburetion, which requires a special control on the dash the pilot can pull, allowing hot exhaust to enter the throat of the carburetor to melt any ice that might form. And form it will, and sometimes with tragic results. One has to constantly be alert for it. A rough running engine is an indication, along with a drop in RPMs. If allowed to build too much, the gas flow may be restricted to the point of the engine starving for fuel. If the engine quits, it is high-ly unlikely to restart again once the ice has formed to that extent. When the air is more saturated with moisture, one must be more alert. This was one thing I was going to have to pay attention to.

Each wing had an 18-gallon fuel tank for a total of 36 gallons. A couple of these gallons had to be deducted as unusable. At nine gallons per hour (GPH) one had a four-hour range max, but little or no reserve. One flies by the clock in planes, especially like this one, and after three hours I would be looking for fuel.

I carried a couple extra five gallon cans to be safe and figured I could set down on a gravel bar somewhere or on the Alcan Highway to replenish. True airspeed was about 100 MPH in this configura-tion. Alaskan models with big tires trued out at closer to 90 MPH. I estimated the trip to take 32 to 35 hours actual flying time, and with the long days I could probably make it in two days, all contingent on the weather. Headwinds or bad weather could extend that time.

I contacted ground control in the tower and got my clearance to taxi to the active runway. My takeoff was uneventful and exhila-rating. I swung over to Interstate 5 and proceeded north. Though I could discern I was moving faster than the cars below, it didn't appear to be by much. This was going to be a long trip.

My first landing ever in a taildragger was in Redding, California. They cleared me to land on the active, and I didn't bother to do a wind check. It was a slightly quartering crosswind from the rear. Upon touching down, I realized quickly I was going to have my hands full. I didn't know the difference between a three-point land-ing and a wheel landing. Whatever I did and however I corrected, I did all the right things, but not without a pucker factor.

The flight was uneventful through Oregon and Washington. I camped on a grass airfield in northern Washington, waited for the FBO to arrive, fueled up, and headed to Abbotsford, British Columbia, to clear Canadian customs.

I must confess I didn't always do this as it was not always convenient. But on this first trip, I did. When I arrived there, I asked the tower where customs was, and they directed me. I walked in and no one was present. There was a phone and a sign that said to call a certain number and get a clearance. I did so and after some questioning I was granted a number, which I wrote on my hand since I couldn't find a piece of paper.

I left there and proceeded slightly east following the Fraser River. I passed Hope, where *Rambo* was filmed with Sylvester Stallone walking across the bridge. Soon I passed Boston Bar. At some point up the Fraser River, I found myself in lowering visibility, going under the wires with orange balls attached and shortly emerged to pass over a town called Clinton.

I picked up the highway to Williams Lake, fueled there, and continued north past Prince George to the town of McKenzie. From there if one followed the highway, the track would go over the Rockies and cross the Peace River picking up mile zero of the Alcan Highway. It was a safer route for sure with a road under you and towns here and there. But it was longer, so I chose the more direct route over very remote country.

I took off from McKenzie and was soon at the foot of Williston Lake. I was astounded at the number of floating logs. The lake appeared unnavigable. It was over 150 miles long, and sitting on the north end was a village called Ingenika. I decided to stop and fuel there, never thinking I would have a problem finding fuel.

Wrong. They were out and hadn't gotten their quota of fuel yet after a long winter. I camped there for the night, but I was concerned. If the winds were favorable I should not have a problem and should make the Alcan Highway where, if I ran short before getting to Watson Lake, I could emergency on the highway and get a ride for fuel. Now I wished I had brought a couple more five-gallon cans of fuel as a safety valve. It was a lesson learned, and I never flew another trip without all the extra cans of fuel my weight and balance allowed.

The Kechika River, which flows northwesterly through the Trench from Sifton pass, had few if any safe places to emergency on. I observed on the map a small village called Fort Ware that maybe could spare me a little extra fuel just for safety.

The wind was about ten knots on my nose. Though this was not too bad, it was making it way more marginal than I wanted. I arrived over the village and circled a couple times low. The runway looked okay, and I could see villagers excitedly running about, looking up, wondering who it might be. I landed and taxied up to a small store and shut down.

Immediately I was surrounded by faces peering in at me with noses pressed against the glass. I got out and said hello. They were all smiles. I headed for the store, and already the owner had come out and was walking toward me. I asked about fuel, and he said he could help me out for $25 a gallon. I had no chamois cloth to strain fuel or funnel with a filter of any kind. Not good. But I had no choice. It was mogas (automotive gas), and though I had no STC (supplemental type certificate, a converted engine) to run auto gas, I figured it was way better than no gas. I bought ten gallons (probably could have done it with five gallons), but I would rather be safe than sorry. It was mixed with oil too.

As it turned out, the trip went smoothly on up through the Trench where I picked up the Alcan Highway into Watson Lake. It was not until I stopped at Beaver Creek, Yukon, for the night, only 20 miles from US Customs and the border, that I ran into trouble. I landed on the little grass field near the Alcan Highway and found a place to tie down. I grabbed my backpack with valuables and my gun and started hiking back toward the village two kilometers away. I was walking down the Alcan with the Canadian customs building to my back.

The next thing I knew, I had a Royal Canadian Mounted Police (RCMP) vehicle racing toward me from the village, lights flashing and siren going. He stopped across from me, stepped out of his vehicle with gun in hand, and commanded me to come to him. I did and he grabbed my gun and threw it into his patrol vehicle. He demanded I drop my pack, and he kicked my legs apart and handcuffed me. I couldn't believe I was being treated this way. I got in the back of his vehicle, and we proceeded down to the customs station less than a half mile away.

We went inside, and they demanded to see my ID and any paperwork. I informed them I had an airplane and had just landed on my way to Alaska. That surprised them. Though the customs station was close to the tiny gravel strip I had landed on, they apparently didn't hear or notice. When they saw me walking, they assumed I was a vagrant and had slipped around them from the Alaska side. I explained about clearing customs with no one present and having been given a number. I was now thankful I had cleared customs, but wait, what was that number they gave me? Of course at that point they asked for it. I showed them my hand, and they laughed.

By now they were beginning to think maybe they had made a mistake, but would check out my story with Abbotsford while I stayed in town. I was planning to stay anyway, and the RCMP graciously offered me a ride to town and to a motel with a shower. He even picked me up within the hour and took me to a place to eat and bought me dinner. He became very hospitable. Next morning early, he picked me up and took me to breakfast. After eating, he took me back down to the customs station. By then they had cleared my story, and I was on my way.

My last main obstacle was clearing customs in the USA. I crossed the border and flew low over our customs station on the highway. There was no official place to land. On return trips I landed on the highway next to customs and cleared there, saving them a trip by car to Northway, Alaska, some 10 to 15 miles away.

Finally, Harold showed up from US Customs and checked me in. It was the beginning of a long friendship since I would be flying many more Pipers up to Alaska and clearing customs with him. I continued on my trip out of Northway, through Mentasta Pass and over Gulkano, cutting across near Glennallen to Lake Louise.

There I picked up the Glenn Highway to Gun Sight where I landed on the highway and taxied into a filling station among the cars to top my tanks off. I was photographed a lot, and I noticed an Alaskan State Trooper on a pay phone standing nearby. He never said a word. I taxied back out on the highway and took off, narrowly missing a motorhome heading in the opposite direction and hidden out of sight by a large dip in the highway.

I proceeded down Chickaloon Pass into Anchorage and finally across Turnagain Arm to Soldotna. Total flying hours were approximately 33. Never had I been so happy to see the Soldotna airport. It was a long and arduous trip, but in no way did it qualify me as an Alaskan bush pilot.

That would take many more years of flying on the edge, in and out of extreme uncharted landing areas, many never landed on before. I would have to learn to handle tricky winds on narrow exposed ridges and high obstacles on each end of a landing area. There would be weather judgments to make, as well as varied terrain to land in and get out of. I had barely begun on the broad learning curve that would challenge me to the fullest.

CHAPTER 15

BUSH SKY TRUCK

As good as Piper Super Cubs are in the Alaskan bush, they don't haul bulky and extremely heavy loads. While shuttling all those Pipers from California to Alaska, I had the good fortune to come across a very good but old and high-time DeHavilland DHC-2 Beaver plane sitting forlorn on wheels at the Northway airport near the US Customs station. It had a for sale sign on it pricing it at $35,000.

I inquired inside, and a friendly fellow immediately took me outside to the plane. After getting in the pilot's seat, pumping the wobble pump (a manual pump that primes the engine), setting the throttle, and turning on the mags, he stepped outside, told me to stand clear, and proceeded to pull the massive propeller. After just a slight pull, bingo, the huge radial engine coughed and sprang to life. After the smoke cleared, I stood in awe listening to the engine idle.

I was sold. We agreed on the price, and I told him I would be back in a few days with the cash to pick it up. I made the offer based on a check ride. I would have to find someone to fly me up there.

In those days, an Alaskan's word was his bond. I remember selling a 26-foot Halibut boat to a fellow from Homer for $32,500. I was asking $35,000. After the demonstration, he opened his trunk and pulled out a freezer pack filled with wads of hundreds, fifties, and twenties.

I handed it back and said, "Sorry, no deal."

He asked what I would take. I told him, and he handed the wad back to me and said deal and he would be back Monday with the balance to get the boat. With that he left. No paperwork. No receipt. Deal done on a handshake and our word.

He showed up Monday with the amount difference, and while hooking up the boat I handed him back $800 for the overage I'd counted in the freezer pack.

Several days had passed since my arrival back in Soldotna, and I headed out to the airport to talk to anyone who might have the time to fly me up to Northway so I could get that plane. When I got to the airport that morning, I was startled and elated to see the Beaver sitting on the ramp. I couldn't believe it. I figured the owner had flown it down for me. I fully expected to find him inside MARC, the local FBO on the field.

I stepped in and looked around and only saw familiar MARC faces. I inquired about the plane, and no one knew anything. I called the Northway office. The fellow answered, and I asked him who I was to pay for the plane and thanked him for bringing it down.

He said I had already paid him. I said no, I had the cash still in my pocket and was looking for someone to take me up there when I found it already delivered.

He then asked me if I were so and so. I reminded him who I was and about our conversation. He apologized then and said someone from Soldotna had arrived a couple days after I left, and he just assumed it was me and sold the airplane.

I was devastated. I could see how that could happen with both of us from Soldotna. Also, money in hand was better than an "I'll be back."

I hung up and went outside and placed one of my cards in the crack of the Beaver door after writing that I thought that it was my plane and that I had made a verbal deal for it.

That night I got a call from a very nice gentleman who owned it and he apologized for the mistake and timing. He, too, had come up the Alaskan Highway the week before and saw the plane and wanted it and had just gone there with the money to do the deal, not knowing about me.

The seller didn't remember my name and just assumed it was me since the other buyer was from Soldotna too. But the gentleman assured me he would keep my card, and if and when he ever sold it, I would be the first person he would call. I thanked him for that. Generally Alaskans have a code of honor seldom encountered in the lower 48.

With that deal off the table, I knew I needed to focus. My dad had no use for golf but used to tell a joke about the golfer who overshot the green and landed in a sand trap square on top of an ant hill. After several swings and misses, picking up sand and ants with each miss, the golfer readied for another swing. Of the two ants left in the sand, one turned to the other and yelled, "If we don't get on the ball, we're next." If I didn't get on the ball, I would run out of my time limit for leaving the Super Cubs parked in California.

Over the course of the next couple months, I busied myself with flying commercially down to Sacramento and flying another plane north. Each trip was an adventure. Only on one occasion did I find someone adventurous enough to fly down with me and fly one of them back. It was one of the most fun trips I have made and it was a joy to have a friend along in another plane for camaraderie.

Dick Page was an excellent pilot. He was a graduate of Moody Bible Flight School in Tennessee, where I had made his acquaintance. I stopped there often to refuel on flights between the Midwest Correct Craft warehouse in Angola, Indiana, and the factory in Orlando, Florida. Neither of us had any idea that someday we both would end up together in Soldotna, Alaska, of all places. Dick became a full-time pilot and mechanic at MARC.

Well within the time limit agreed to, I managed to get the whole fleet to Alaska and had already begun to sell several of them. The very first one I flew up, which was the oldest and had the highest time on airframe and engine, I lost to a scoundrel due to a land deal gone sour. I found out that not all Alaskans were cut out of the same cloth. That is another story to tell but is best left untold.

The others sold readily, some on the high side and some on the low side. In all I ended up with enough gain to own a couple outright to keep and use. One I put on floats and the other on wheels and skis. Of course I loaded them both up with most Alaskan mods. Another year went by when out of the blue I received a call from a fellow who asked me if I remembered him. He was the one who had bought the DHC-2 Beaver out from under me.

My heart skipped a beat as I told him that I remembered. He said if I were still interested in buying it, he would sell it to me for the same price he had paid plus the cost of the hydraulic skis he had added.

We met at the airport. I looked the plane over and then asked him if he minded telling me why he was selling. He said he wanted to buy a smaller plane like a Cub, and he understood a fellow had bought a bunch of them in the lower 48 and was offering good deals.

My heart again skipped a beat. I came right back at him and said, "How about two?" I don't remember exactly how that deal went down, but almost every sale of one of those planes was special.

CHAPTER 16

WHEELS TO FLOATS

I taught myself how to fly the Beaver. The only thing I needed help on was how to start it using that wobble pump. I figured if I could start it, I could fly it by now, due to my flying experience. I was right. It flew like a big Super Cub. I put hundreds of hours on it with wheels, but I longed to put it on a set of good floats, for that is what makes a Beaver one of the world's premier bush planes. It has few equals. But first I had to get my float rating.

I had flown in float planes in Alaska on several occasions and always watched carefully and asked lots of questions. From the right seat on occasion, I would even pilot one down to a landing, but until one goes to floatplane school and learns the many nuances necessary to fly safely, one is best not self-taught.

After going to Seattle and achieving my float rating at Kenmore Air Harbor, the premier Beaver floatplane base with a float flying school, I decided to purchase a used set of EDO 2000 floats (the floats of choice for Super Cubs) for one of the two remaining Super Cubs I had. I flew to Four Corners near Wasilla, Alaska, and landed on a small strip there to have the float fittings welded on, including lifting eyes located on top of the wing roots to easily lift the plane to install and uninstall the floats.

This is the very plane I flew over to Canada to trade for the EDO 4930 floats for my Beaver.

The Super Cub would be less expensive to build time and experience on floats with. Plus, the Super Cub was a performer and could fill in until I could find a good set of EDO 4930 floats for the Beaver. No other float performed on a Beaver like those, but they were both scarce and expensive, even back then. The cost of a new set was astronomical.

I finally found a set in Calgary, Alberta. They were spendy, but the exchange rate was favorable for me with US funds. We agreed on a deal sight unseen, and part of the deal was that they would deliver an Otter they had sold to Ketchum Aircraft in Anchorage and then have their pilot come down to Soldotna and fly my Beaver back to Calgary to fit the floats.

But the main part of the deal was a trade. I traded my Super Cub on floats for the floats for the Beaver. My part of the bargain included me flying the Super Cub on floats from Alaska to Calgary, British Columbia—no small task. I had no idea how hard that would be, flying from lake to lake, finding fuel, and trying to clear customs. Frankly, I gave up on customs. There is a lot of empty and remote space between Soldotna, Alaska, and Calgary, British Columbia.

About the first of July, I received a call informing me the floats were installed on the Beaver, and it was ready for pick up. They had agreed as part of the deal (I should have learned my lesson by now) to have a check pilot down at the Bearspaw Reservoir to give me some pointers on flying a Beaver on floats.

This reservoir was created by damming up the Bow River. It sits at about 3,500-feet elevation and is west-northwest of Calgary. I was ready to go. I had removed the Borer propeller and reinstalled the standard Piper propeller (which was better for speed and less expensive to include in the trade) and loaded my survival gear and four five-gallon cans of gas. I fueled all the tanks and headed out.

I lifted off Longmere Lake and turned northerly. I flew over Anchorage, skirting the Terminal Control Area, headed up past Chickaloon, and landed at Lake Louise near Glennallen where I stayed for the night and topped off my fuel. From there I planned a slight diversion up to Dawson City, Yukon, which I had never visited. I landed on the famous Yukon River and taxied to shore.

I had called ahead, and customs met me at the Yukon River and gave me a clearance. I pitched my tent and enjoyed the midnight sun. A walk on the boardwalk and a visit to Diamond Tooth Girty's was in order. Early next morning, with the plane fueled with the extra fuel I brought along, I figured I still could make Whitehorse and land on Schwatka Lake. The lake was actually a reservoir made by damming up the famous Yukon River just below Miles Canyon, where so many of the Klondikers died or lost all their outfits trying to negotiate the rapids and whirlpools. I knew it would be close on fuel depending on winds.

I followed Canadian Route 2 from Dawson City through Stewart Crossing, Pelly Crossing, and down to the huge Lake Laberge made famous by the Klondikers seeking gold. Robert Service in his famous poem, "The Cremation of Sam McGee," told an interesting story that related to this lake.

I came up with my own shortened version that goes like this:

There are strange things done in the midnight sun by the pilots who fly so bold,

the Arctic trails have their secret tales that would make the FAA's blood run cold. The Northern Lights have seen queer sights, but the queerest they ever did see, was the night in a swamp by the Holitna, yours truly landed in a tree.

I had veered east slightly from the road to fly more over Lake Lebarge to sightsee and for safety. By the time I was down toward the south end of the lake, with my right tank already dry, the ball on the left sight gauge was lying at the bottom, only occasionally bouncing.

Then it happened. The motor sputtered and grew silent. I was too far out of Whitehorse to wiggle wings and try to get the last drops out of the tanks. I simply turned toward the western shoreline nearest to the road and set it down. I exited, grabbed my paddle, and paddled the plane to shore.

After securing the tail of the floats in the weeds at the edge of the water, I grabbed two empty five-gallon fuel cans and started hiking through the woods toward the road.

It was less than a half mile. Traffic was scarce. I finally flagged down a truck driver and hitched a ride into the outskirts of Whitehorse to a filling station. I topped the cans off and started walking back up Highway 2 toward the lake. In short order I was picked up by a friendly Canadian driver going my way who took me near to where I came out of the woods. I failed to mark exactly where I had exited the woods, so had some trouble and a bit more walking before I arrived at the plane.

Those gas cans, at 30 pounds each, were growing heavy. I fueled and headed on into Schwatka Lake that evening and camped. In the morning I fueled up and taxied way back up the lake almost into Miles Canyon where I could see whirlpools in order to make it off with that slow-turning, high-pitched propeller. I cleared the dam and turned southeast to Skagway, my next stop.

I flew Canadian Highway 1, the Alcan Highway, east a ways until I could turn southerly at Marsh Lake and fly down to Carcross. I thought about the Disney film *Never Cry Wolf*, which used Carcross as one of the towns.

From there I flew to Bennett Lake, made famous by the Klondike gold rushers who built all kinds of craft to shorten and speed up their journeys into the gold fields. When they would have to build a craft, it made sense to do so on the south end of Bennett where plenty of wood could be found. Too, after climbing the dangerous Chilkoot Trail over the Pass, they needed time to recuperate and take stock of their situation.

I had always dreamed of flying this trail, and here I was going down it toward the sea. I arrived at Dyea, the civilized jumping off point for the gold seekers for the dangerous trek up the Chilkoot Trail. From there it was a short hop over to the Skagway boat harbor. I landed just outside the harbor and taxied in among the myriad of boats. I found an empty spot at the end of a pier and tied up for the night. It was a fun night walking the boardwalks and taking in a Soapy Smith show.

The next morning after breakfast, I headed out again, this time down Taiya Inlet to Chilkoot Inlet and on into the Juneau, Alaska, airport. The float pond was adjacent to the runway. I fueled up, had some lunch, and headed out again, this time for Wrangell. I fueled there and prepared to penetrate the great Canadian wilderness, heading cross-country through some of the most hostile territory I have ever flown. It seemed so daunting. No flight plan was possible.

Clearing Canadian Customs was also impossible since there were no points of entry going up the Stikine River. I eventually crossed the Cassiar Highway many miles inland and proceeded on a southeasterly course, having to stop on a remote lake and utilize the extra gas. I believe the lake was Babine Lake. From there I kept angling until I arrived at Stuart Lake and its small town of Fort St. James.

There I saw a crowd of afternoon bathers enjoying some sunshine on a Canadian holiday coincident with our Independence Day holiday, July fourth. I taxied to shore and got a big crowd of onlookers. Several were very helpful and even took my empty cans and went to a station, filling them several times, allowing me to top off my tanks and fill my spare gas cans.

The trip through Prince George and east through the Wells Gray Provincial Park, Jasper National Park, and on down to the town of Golden was uneventful other than some moderate turbulence in the mountains. I turned easterly again and followed the Trans-Canada Highway through the rugged Rocky Mountains and Banff National Park, making a slight diversion to land on one of the clearest and most beautiful lakes I have ever seen, Lake Louise. It was so clear one could see straight down, over 100 feet, to the bottom of the lake.

I didn't stay long as I was afraid I would attract too much attention, and headed on toward Calgary. (That lake by the way was off limits to float plane traffic at the time.) I found Bearspaw Reservoir, which was about 3,500 feet elevation and landed on a hot, beautiful day at the predetermined spot. I had called them from Stewart Lake and gave them an ETA, and sure enough they were there waiting.

I signed my Super Cub over to them, loaded my things into my Beaver sitting on those beautiful 4930 EDO floats, and asked who was going to check me out. Sure enough, their check pilot was a no-show, and here I was heading out to fly a Beaver on floats with no prior take offs or landings and no pointers as to flaps, etc. I was disappointed and almost camped there to wait until the next day, but with the long, lingering Northern Hemisphere light, I decided to push on.

The density altitude was high, which would make it more challenging for the plane to get lift. I cranked up and started taxiing out. I pushed the right rudder and the plane veered left, just the opposite direction it should have gone. I pushed the left rudder and it turned right. I turned to see if they had departed, and sure enough there were no vehicles at the boat ramp and only taillights heading out of the dirt access road.

I checked the other controls and they seemed fine. I did a run-up (bringing the RPMs of the engine up while braked to make final checks) and checked carb heat (a separate heater for the carburetor to warm the air). Satisfied, I poured the coals to her and tried to get the plane on step or get enough lift to get in the air. I knew the density altitude was going to hurt performance, but this was ridiculous. I ran a long ways to no avail. Fishermen were mad and flipping me off. The plane just wouldn't get up on the step. What was wrong?

I taxied back slowly trying to get my wits around me, and then realized I had gotten distracted and forgot to release the carb heat. That would make a big difference. I also put on ten degrees of flaps and went for it again. I had topped off all my gas cans, which included a bunch more I had sent back with their pilot. With the additional gas and the heavy landing gear with huge tires and wheels, I was quite heavy. I knew with the load and heat, my performance would be marginalized.

But sure enough, as I came in with the power I could feel a big difference in performance. It rolled over onto the step and I was flying. I turned northerly and followed the highway toward Red Deer and then Edmonton. I veered west slightly and went around the city, but I could see darkness was overtaking me. I had to find a place to land shortly where I could set up a good approach and do my first landing. Never in my wildest imagination would I have thought I would be doing my first landing in my Beaver on floats in the dark, but that is exactly what happened.

By the time I got to Lesser Slave Lake, the last sign of light flickered out on the horizon to the west, and I was flying in the dark. I got Air Canada on the radio and explained my predicament whereupon I was informed that no VFR (visual flight rules) were allowed at night in Canada. I apologized for my ignorance and begged for a local pilot that knew the lake and could recommend at least what side to land on and if there were any obstructions.

I circled a bit while he came to the station. Soon he was on the radio telling me not to worry about obstructions, other than the possibility of overzealous fishermen, and to land on the south side of the lake and I would find a campground there.

I set my altimeter to the current setting and began my descent. It was a large lake and gave me ample room to make a safe power-on landing, a technique one uses for glassy water, which is like landing on a mirror with no reference to where the water is. Night landings were the same scenario. When I got to where I thought the water was close, I flicked on my landing lights and kept my descent about 1 to 200 feet per minute until I felt the water under my floats and immediately cut power and floated to a stop.

My heart was pounding, and I was so thankful I was down safely. I taxied slowly to shore where I saw what appeared to be campfires. Soon I was beached and secured for the night. I pitched my tent and woke to a beautiful sunrise. I built a fire, heated some coffee, and had a breakfast bar. Soon I was auguring into the sky heading for mile zero of the Alcan Highway.

I proceeded past Fort St. John 50 miles north and landed for fuel at Charlie Lake. No one was there, but the pump was unlocked and there was a clipboard to write your name and mailing address, with a spot to mark the fuel measurement at the beginning and the end with the total number of gallons. I thought that was pretty cool and trusting.

The remainder of the trip was like clockwork. Harold the customs agent came to me on some designated lake near the customs station at Northway, Alaska to check me in. I made it to Soldotna uneventfully, and sure enough in several weeks I received a bill for my gas on Charlie Lake (and yes, I immediately sent a check). With this Beaver on floats, I was on the threshold of a whole new set of adventures.

CHAPTER 17

FRANKLIN GRAHAM

My move to Alaska led to a loss of contact with my family for several years, until 1994 when my father ran into Franklin Graham at a sunrise service held at SeaWorld in Orlando. Afterward, my dad approached him and asked if he could consider going to Alaska and checking on me as they had lost contact.

The Graham family's history with the Meloons went back a long way, especially between my Uncle Walt and the Billy Graham Evangelistic Association. Dad offered to reimburse Franklin for expenses for the trip.

Franklin declined the reimbursement and said he needed no excuse to go to Alaska since it had a warm spot in his heart. Yes, he would go and check on me.

Later that Spring found the whole Franklin Graham family flying to Alaska. They landed in Soldotna and rented a car. I lived only a mile from the airport and was under a boat in the driveway working on the bottom when they arrived. Someone hadn't liked the competition I gave them flying fishers in remote and had used a 12-gauge shotgun on the bottom, turning it into a giant sieve. I was repairing the holes when I heard a car door slam and saw the fancy city shoes of someone approaching.

Who was this dude? I thought it might be the FAA, Fish and Game, or the IRS.

Then a voice said, "Does Ralph Meloon live here?"

I responded, "Maybe he does and maybe he doesn't. Who wants him?"

He announced, "I'm Franklin Graham."

And that was the beginning of an enduring relationship that has grown stronger through the years.

The very next day began a series of adventures that continue to this day. We left early in the morning for Wolverine Creek across Cook Inlet. In the first load—since I couldn't accommodate the whole family in my C185 on floats—I took Jane, Will (their oldest son), and Cissie, the youngest and only daughter, and hands down the best fisher of them all.

I returned to get Franklin, rebel boy Roy, and Edward, a future West Point grad and Army Ranger. What fun this family was to entertain. In fact, they entertained me. We fished and fished in this remote hole, and those were the days when mainly local fishers came to load up their year supply of sockeye without the hordes of chartered lower-48ers you see today.

Over the years I have concluded that the worst offenders of Alaska's Fish and Game laws are the local yokels better known as sourdoughs. Of course that would not be me. Why, I would never tie off a gill net between my floats and taxi around in a pond loaded with fresh sockeye salmon struggling to end their lives in the salmon circle of life.

We began fishing, and it wasn't long before the local bush residents (AKA brown bears) started arriving for their meals. They were big, grumpy, mostly brown, liked to fight, and had voracious appetites. Even though we had guns to protect ourselves and knew how to use them, we always drew them with reluctance, conceding to the bears their rightful place in the fishing hierarchy at fishing holes.

With our limits filling fast and the light waning, I departed with Cissie, Will, and Jane. I had asked Franklin to move around the cove across the creek and wait for me to return. Since it would be oh-dark-thirty, I did not want to have to navigate the boulder-strewn area between where I landed and where they now stood.

As predicted, when I arrived back the light was gone. Yes in Alaska it is not uncommon to find bush pilots landing and taking off in the dark, a practice discouraged by the FAA. In fact, they suggest a pilot caught in darkness on floats to land at the nearest lighted airport and figure on an expensive bill to fix the floats.

I taxied in and made a slow turn, looking in the specific direction I had told them to go. They were not there. I turned again and looked and still no sign. Maybe someone had arrived and fished while I was gone and had room and took them out for me.

I decided to make one last 360 degree turn to look and bingo: I saw a silver flash in my landing light and taxied toward it. It was Roy with a hooked fish fighting for its life. I bumped a couple of boulders but made my way up to them in the dark. I asked Franklin why they hadn't hiked over to the other spot, and he pointed his flashlight toward the creek.

Sure enough, in the spotlight we saw over a dozen pairs of eyes staring at us. It didn't take a rocket scientist to know what was behind those eyes. Franklin had made the right decision. I told them to jump in and let's go, that the adventure was just beginning. My, was it ever. From Cook Inlet in South Central Alaska to the beautiful Lake Clark/Iliamna region west of the Alaska Range in southwest Alaska, we have flown, hiked, camped, fished, hunted, and wrecked. How could you ask for anything more?

Stories about Franklin and Jane and their family are almost too numerous to recount, like the time we were all fishing together at a bear-gathering hole when Jane's foot became stuck between a rock and a hard spot with a hovering mama bear hardly ten feet away. The mama bear pounded a large boulder menacingly while her cub, without invitation, decided to come sit and fish beside Jane. Or the time when we came up a narrow, weed-choked bear trail leading from the lower Newhalen River back to our airplanes parked at the Iliamna airport. We were loaded down with our limit of Sockeye salmon in packs on our back when two small brown bear cubs happened across our trail just ahead. They were soon followed by a protective mom who suddenly appeared, blocking our path, shaking her head back and forth, and chomping her gigantic canines together while drooling pints of saliva. Or the time, while brown bear hunting with close friend and companion Doctor Dick Furman, a huge Alaskan moose lost nearly two feet of antler spread from the time I called it in until the moment Franklin lined up to take him down.

"Take him," I said.

From our stealthy position we could see a rutting bull moose hammering a spruce tree only 50 yards away, its antlers swishing back and forth amongst the many branches. The powerful rifle went *bang* as Franklin lowered the boom on the largest member of the deer family. It collapsed in a heap with one deadeye shot, after which we leaped up to move toward the spot. The closer we got, the more unsure I was that it was the same huge bull I called earlier. Meanwhile, Doc Furman found his way down to us to excitedly tell us our big bull was about 100 yards away watching the whole scenario. Dejectedly we pulled out our measuring tape to confirm our suspicion that this indeed was not our bull, but an imposter who decided to join the party and was just shy of being legal.

After a surgery-like dressing of a moose (the Doc's signature on it), we flew out on my PA12 with the whole load in one trip to Soldotna to turn it in to Fish and Game. There, "Take him, don't take him," took on a kind of hilarious tone. It resulted in a court appearance before the magistrate in Kenai and a payment to the State of the fine.

"Your fault, you pay the fine," my wife said.

I tried to convince her I said, "Don't take him" and Franklin just didn't hear the "don't." After all, Jane had been trying to convince him to get hearing aids. But no one believed my story, so I paid up. Well, mistakes can be made, and they are. The right thing to do is confront them head-on with the truth, and we did. In the end, it paid off with the bagging of a gigantic bull in the upper 60-inch class which now proudly hangs on a wall in the General (meeting hall) at the Operation Heal Our Patriots Project (OHOP) headquarters in Port Alsworth. And that is another story to tell someday.

Franklin with his huge bull moose taken in one of the remotest regions of Alaska.

Of course, Franklin also had a huge heart for the people of Alaska. It came in the form of spiritual transformations like Alaska has never seen before. Gradually, as our Alaskan adventures were lived out (safely though not always smoothly) God laid on Franklin's heart a vision for needs all over Alaska, from the main cities to the smallest remote villages—a vision which has changed its spiritual landscape. From new churches in remote villages, to new homes replacing burned out ones, to a whole new project, OHOP, ministering to the many needs of America's broken warriors (true patriots, both husbands and wives), the gospel of Jesus Christ is permeating this vast, last remote frontier of America.

CHAPTER 18

USAF INTERDICTION

S eptember 11, 2001 will forever be etched in the memory of millions of Americans. Most can share exactly what they were doing on that fateful day when America came under attack by a bunch of jihadists.

It was also the beginning of our main hunting season in Alaska. Being a registered big game guide, this time of the year always finds me out in the killing fields, flying clients to and from remote hunting camps in pursuit of either caribou, moose, or brown bear.

For the last several years, I had been flying with and for Lake Clark Air of Port Alsworth doing outfitted drop hunts for our normal bookings, plus a large number of Cabela hunts. Though I still had holdings on the Holitna River about 100 miles north where I had independently guided hunting and fishing clients for quite a number of years, I had migrated further south to the beautiful and more pristine Lake Clark region to live near and work with Glen Alsworth and his company, Lake Clark Air, flying, outfitting, and guiding.

It is strenuous and dangerous to work alone, and that is what I had done for many years with no backup. The camaraderie of working with fellow Christians doing work I loved while enjoying their support and backup was beyond description. We functioned like a well-oiled machine, and I was flying with such gifted bush pilots as Mark Lang, Glen Alsworth Sr. himself, his able son Glenie, his son-in-law Leo Fowler, and several additional competent pilots.

I asked Glen Sr. one day how many times he had crashed. He said, "Me, crash? Why would I crash? I pay guys to." After surviving several crashes myself, I was hoping for some admitted company in my mishaps. While I didn't get any confessions from Glen, it bears pointing out that one generally cannot fly on the edge like we do in Alaska, carrying all kinds of loads and landing in different places everyday with constantly changing wind conditions, without some mishaps.

Glen and I were ptarmigan (Alaska's state bird) hunting one day at a place we called Ptar Two. We name all our drop-off places and share the coordinates with fellow pilots for the safety of our clientele. Ptar was short for ptarmigan. When we first landed there years prior, we probably scared up a bunch of ptarmigan and aptly named it Ptar. The number two was added since we already had used that name on another location.

We had been shuttling hunters from the village of Koliganek who had just landed on a flight from Anchorage. We had some time to spare and decided to hunt. We had just been startled by a large nine-foot-plus brown bear that had exploded out of an alder thicket we were circling, and we had nothing but a .22 rifle and a .410 shotgun. We were hunting for ptarmigan and had seen a flock fly into this thicket. We already had a couple of birds in our pocket. I had gotten them with the .410 after missing a few.

Glen was carrying the .22 and as of yet hadn't gotten a clear shot. I guess he was determined to show me how it was done. I heard one shot on the other side of the alders where he went. When we met on the far end, he had three birds in hand. He never said a word. We sat for a few minutes and started talking, and I remember discussing how many takeoffs and landings we had already done that day and none in the same place and most on the tundra. A couple dozen as I remember. There are pilots in the lower 48 that do well to do that many landings and takeoffs in a year on paved runways.

Mark Lang and I would often talk when we had downtime while flying hunters. Naturally we would discuss where we had been that day, how hard it was to land or take off from a particular spot depending on winds and loads, and invariably the discussion would end up on picking the spots to set camps. Mark and I were in total agreement. When it came to yarding out a camp that Glen had chosen and named, places like Iffy, Short, Lumpy, or Roll, we always either flipped a coin as to who would do it or fight over not doing it. To sum up, Glen had a knack for landing in places that just were not the top of our wish list.

It so happened on September 10, the day before that fateful day, I was commissioned to yard a camp out of one of Glen's infamous tight spots. It was late in the day, and there just was no way I could safely haul two hunters and their camp off that hill simultaneously. I told the one fellow who volunteered to stay that I probably couldn't make it back that night and get him.

He was ecstatic. He loved it there. They had been listening to wolves howl every night, and the weather was forecast to be clear and cold. He told me to not bother trying to get back. He had a block of cheese and some crackers, his sleeping bag, air mattress, a tarp to wrap up in, and his rifle.

The next morning when I flew off the beach in front of my cabin, nine miles down the lake from Port Alsworth, to rendezvous at the Farm (the affectionate name for Glen's home), I began to hear on my VHF radio, "If you are flying a plane in Alaska, land immediately." This message was going continuously every few minutes. I must have heard it a half dozen times by the time I reached the

Farm. I landed on Runway 5 Left on the last third of the runway and fast taxied to the gas pumps for fuel.

Glen came out and met me, and I asked him what was going on. He told me America was under attack and we had to park the planes. All airspace in America was closed until further notice. I informed Glen that I had a poor chap out on a hill 60 miles north with next to nothing to survive on, and I had to get him. He agreed and mentioned there was no way he could make the trip since the FAA knew he was informed about the closure. That left it up to me to rescue him.

We had no way of knowing that it would be four long days before the airspace would be opened again in Alaska when the FAA recognized there had to be exceptions to the rule. There were unhappy campers left to fend for themselves in numerous camps all over Alaska with no way to get word to them about the circumstances.

I fueled up, jumped in my Super Cub, and was off for my hunter. I climbed as usual to at least 1,000 feet above the lake for gliding room to the shore in case of motor failure. I would need additional altitude as I progressed toward our client via Tutna Lake.

By the time I was approaching Tutna Lake, I was observing two black dots dropping like rocks out of the sky in front of me. I had no idea that the Air Force was so serious they would scramble a couple of fighters to run me down. In fact, I had no idea they could see me so low, but see me they did. They flew past me very fast. I tried to look back over my shoulder to see where they went, but to no avail.

I was now starting to overfly Tutna Lake, and suddenly they were beside me, one on my left and the other on my right at the same altitude. They had slowed down as slow as they could and still didn't have much time to get my attention to wave me down as they flew by, but wave they did, thumbs down. I wagged my wings at them, smiled, and played dumb.

They shot straight up then and looped back behind me to press closer the second time and impress on me how important it was to land. I cut power so they would pass quickly, headed for the hard deck (ground or tree tops), turned toward Mesa Mountain off my right wing, and flew up a small river that flowed out of the mountains. I never saw them again after observing them climbing and heading northwest toward Norton Sound.

I learned later that Glennie and another pilot for Lake Clark Air had also been flying that day and were passing Tutna Lake going in the opposite direction when they noticed the fighters drop out of the sky and make some maneuvers.

I turned back on course, stayed on the hard deck, and headed across the Mulchatna River for the hill he was stranded on. When I landed, I jumped out and encouraged him to move quickly. He wanted to know what was going on. I told him America was under attack. He looked oddly at me and asked, "What have you been smoking?" I assured him nothing and said we had to go quick.

We jumped in and headed for my cabin to land on the beach. No way were we going back to the Farm by plane and landing. Later I took him by boat down the lake to deliver him to our base.

I was just about to turn in for the night when the phone rang. I heard an unfamiliar voice on the other end asking me if I was the owner of N9578P.

I hesitantly answered yes with my heart pounding. The person introduced himself as an investigator for the FAA. He said he received a report that N9578P was observed in closed airspace, and under the circumstances of a national emergency, I could very well have to forfeit my plane.

As a guide in Alaska, being under the threat of losing my plane, depending on the infraction, was not usually a real threat. But this was the Feds. I was speechless for a moment and then returned the threat. I informed him that when I finished lighting a match to my plane, they wouldn't want to bother confiscating it.

Then I thought I heard a snicker. Then another. The person on the other end was beginning to come apart with laughter.

I was furious when I recognized the voice. It was Franklin! He had used a handkerchief to cover the phone. He was beginning to worry I would carry out my threat and demolish my plane. Simply put, I had been pranked by a preacher.

To my knowledge there has never been an event of this magnitude that so affected bush flying in Alaska. Oh, we have had some temporary obstacles, mainly due to weather conditions that have put a wrinkle in our flying, such as an early freeze-up or earlier than usual heavy snowfall. I remember while sheep hunting in the eastern Chugach mountains east of Anchorage a huge snowfall occurred that stranded sheep hunters all over Alaska necessitating Fish and Game to relax the rules for use of helicopters in hunting so stranded hunters could be rescued. In Alaska helicopters are forbidden to be used for any kind of sport hunting; they are too easy to land and shoot from, or prepare to hunt almost anywhere near game. I was hunting with my dear friend and fellow sheep hunter Loren Flagg and we were prepared to tough it out and did. But many couldn't.

Another time an early freeze-up caught me far out in southwestern Alaska with a group of successful hunters while flying floats and I woke up to find my Cessna 185 completely frozen in on a pond we were hunting from. I literally had to take a chain saw and cut around my floats to free the plane, crank up, and slowly taxi ahead, breaking ice and making a path to take off. When I arrived in Soldotna, the lakes there were frozen and one had no idea how thick. I touched down tentatively and fortunately broke through without breaking anything or flipping. What I had to do to rescue my stranded hunters is another story for another book, but here in Alaska during 9/11 we had outfitted hunters stranded all over the hills and valleys hunting caribou, moose, and bear, with no way to communicate with them much less check on them almost daily, which is what we normally do to see if they have meat to remove or need any additional supplies. Needless to say, we had some very upset hunters when we finally had a relaxation of the no-fly regulation four days later.

CHAPTER 19

UPSIDE DOWN
IN A HOLE

I learned on one occasion that when the guiding season is over as far as clients go, even if you have a few extra days left to hunt, just pack up, go home, and enjoy the finish of an accident-free season (uh, if it was one). But no, that's not me. I was spreading wet tents and gear out all over the front room of my remote cabin to let them dry when there was a knock at my door.

I grabbed my handgun and stuck it in my belt and headed for the door. One never knows in the bush who might be standing there, friend or foe. It was Rich Dykema, a long-time friend whom I had met years ago in California. We realized we both had a love for Alaska and developed a quick bond. He had a friend with him, and they excitedly shared what they had discovered across the lake near the Lower Taz.

The lake southwest of our lake, Lake Clark, is Six Mile Lake, where the Native village Non Dalton sits. It has a world-class fishing river that flows into it called the Tazimina, the headwaters of which are upper and lower Tazimina. Sitting just west of this area is the infamous weather-maker Roadhouse Mountain. Snuggled down low in a bottom area were bull moose, and lots of them. They had congregated to battle it out for some cows in the area.

The catch was Rich and his friend had no bush plane like a Super Cub to land back in that country to get near this treasure trove of animals. Their C180 was not capable of landing safely on the few ridges in the area.

They caught me at a weak moment and with the words, "Huge bulls, just across the lake, no brainer, fun, friends," ringing in my ears, I went to bed that night. The next morning I was all in. We packed our gear, and I flew the first hunter up to look for the bulls and find a place to land nearby. We readily found both, and I set up an approach and crunched into the side of a hill bouncing up on top. We unloaded quickly and I left to pick up the other fellow. They put the finishing touches on setting up the camp while I secured the plane the best I could, though it was somewhat exposed on the ridge.

After a roaring campfire cookout during which we observed our trail of smoke wafting lazily across the canyon, we noticed movement that turned out to be three brown bears, a sow and two very large grown cubs. While black bears generally kick their young out of the nest after the first year, the grizzly and brown bear species generally stay united for one to three years, and some have been known to stay together longer.

I remember one late evening encounter in which I confronted three very large bears ambling along until they saw me struggling with a load of caribou meat and a rack. Because they were upwind of me and couldn't catch my scent, they immediately came charging toward me at a terrifying speed, closing the gap so fast I hardly had time to get my rifle up and in position to try and stop them. I was shaking. I couldn't see them in my scope. I decided to let go with a shot in front of them, hoping the sound would slow them down and cause them to reconsider.

It worked. I immediately put another shell in the chamber and was wishing I had a semi-auto and not a bolt action with so many so close. They began to circle me, standing up occasionally and looking my way, trying to figure me out. When they got downwind and picked up my scent, they thought differently about their quest and sauntered off.

That was the night I couldn't find my camp (years before handy GPS) as I had set it up in a slight depression and in the stark, treeless tundra could not make a visual on it or my plane and had to spike camp laying on a pile of red meat. Not fun.

Now these three bears were heading straight for our smoke trail, and it was just a matter of minutes before they would encounter it. When they did, they stopped and in unison stood and started sniffing. They wasted no time and headed our way, disappearing in the ravine between us. We grabbed our artillery, loaded up, and waited. We didn't want to shoot and possibly ruin our hunt. We waited what seemed hours with no sign. We sensed they were circling just outside of our camp.

I was concerned for my plane as I had been hauling moose meat, and it probably had the scent of blood. I wished I had brought along a can of Lysol or something to discourage them from tearing into it. On several occasions, bush pilots have come back to their camp to find their plane tattered and torn beyond recognition. Bears will even chew the tires, puncturing them. After some time, we settled in for the night, locked and loaded.

The next morning, we awakened to a stiff breeze coming over and down the mountain that shadowed us just to our north. We grabbed our binoculars and began scoping the valley below. There the moose were, still bunched and sizing one another up menacingly, stiff legged, with massive heads swaying slowly side to side, occasionally locking horns and playing shove-a-war.

We were excited. There was just one problem. That stiff breeze playing over the top of the mountain and spilling down on top of us was picking up and blowing right into their nostrils. It was hunting suicide from our position upwind of the animals to try to put a stalk on them.

Surely they would get our scent and flee the country, especially if we drew close to them. It was then we allowed ourselves to be swayed by our tummies to do a stupid thing. Back at Rich's cabin he had a fresh gallon of milk sitting in his refrigerator doing us no good at all. The more we talked about it, the more we had to have it. That is when Rich jumped in the back of my Super Cub and I jumped in the front for a quickie trip across the lake to satisfy our thirst for milk.

I taxied off the knoll we were perched on so I could get a longer run. It was uphill, and I had gained little momentum by the time we pitched over the top and got on the level. Too, the wind had kicked up more, and we broke ground quickly. However, the mountain was straight ahead and closing fast, and the terrain was rising. The closer I got to the mountain, the more the downslope wind slowed me and began to push me down. I found myself pulling back on the stick more and more to regain lost altitude.

I pulled on ten degrees of flaps and was about to make my turn when I realized how mushy the controls were, how slow I was, and fast approaching a stall. I had to make a split-second decision to either lower the nose and try to keep making the turn and shallow the bank, hoping not to stall-spin into the ground, or just pick a spot straight ahead and set her down.

In that split second of decision, I deserted the turn and aimed the plane straight ahead for a certain collision with the rising terrain. That was not an easy split decision, but one which probably saved our lives and kept us from stall-spinning out of control into the ground. I tried to avoid an alder patch and other obstacles, but ultimately made an unscheduled stop upside down in a rather deep depression.

The disorientation of being upside down was not new to me, though Rich was not as experienced as I. He wasn't sure what to do next. I cut the mags off immediately, as gas was dripping all around us from the wing tanks. We released our seatbelts and fell to the inside roof of the plane and crawled out and away. It was not a pretty sight. The other fellow came running up the hill to see about us, and we all three sat down pretty dejected as we watched our moose hunt terminate in a mangled, expensive heap.

In those days, it was not easy to file flight plans for such impromptu hunts not knowing when they might terminate or where you might end up. So no one had any idea where we were. It was possible to hike out to Lake Clark and follow the shoreline toward the village, all the while looking for a boat that might come by. In the excitement of the moment, I had forgotten about my ELT (emergency locator transmitter). Several hours transpired during which we went back to our camp, ate breakfast, and dejectedly watched the bulls battling away for a harem.

Suddenly we heard a plane coming our way. We grabbed some orange tape to wave until we realized it was a Lake Clark National Park plane. This was one wreck I wasn't going to be able to hide. My dear friend Leon Alsworth, the park ranger, was piloting it. He of course recognized my plane and circled us several times.

I ran up the mountainside to my plane, turned on the master, and got on the radio to talk. He wanted to know if we were okay, and I said yes. Of course he wanted to know what happened, and I suggested a stiff wind blew us over. We didn't elaborate, and he didn't ask, although he was curious what had mowed a path through some of the alder thickets.

We dug a hole in front of the engine, pulled off the prop, tied a rope to the tail wheel, and pulled the plane over onto its wheels. Leon said he would let Glen Alsworth, his uncle, know, and sure enough, Glen came in the 10A Stinson, which we affectionately called "The Green Weenie."

It was embarrassing to watch Glen taxi up the side of that mountain weaving here and there until he came to the hole. He turned slightly and shut down. He had a rope (it kind of looked like a ski rope), and we tied it to his tail wheel and to my tail wheel, and he ski-pulled my plane right up out of that hole onto higher ground.

He asked what I needed, and I said a prop for sure. The crumpled

struts we could brace with duct taped alder branches. The big problem I was concerned about, among several others, was that one of
the spars on one wing was definitely broken loose from the fuselage.
The whole wing flexed backward when you pushed on it and would
jam the flap right into the fuselage.

After Leo, Glen's head of aircraft maintenance, arrived with
the prop and a couple other items and helped shore up a couple of
things, along with putting the replacement prop on and taking the
flap off that was jamming into the fuselage, I taxied down the mountain to camp and prepare to takeoff on the ridge and head straight
to Lake Clark Air at Port Alsworth.

I was pretty apprehensive, flying the plane as banged up as it
was. I was concerned especially with a broken spar. I asked Glen
what he thought about it. He always had a way of cutting to the
chase with his thoughts and words. He looked at me. "Well, the
wing has two spars, doesn't it?"

I earlier had walked off my potential takeoff path lengthwise on
the ridge. There was a series of three hills with depressions between
them, and I figured I could easily get off by the second one. I didn't
look past that point and wished I had. They had brought me a spare
prop that, unbeknownst to me, was a 58-inch pitch off a Stinson. I
was accustomed to using a Borer prop with 42-inch pitch.

I rolled and rolled and thought I would never get airborne. Off
the first rise, through the depression to the top of the next one, off
of it and through the next depression, then up and over the last one,
and not until I was on the downhill side of it did I finally get air
under my tires.

If I could have jerked on some flaps to help me break ground,
that would have been a plus. But I had never flown a Cub using
one flap, and I left well enough alone, though that last hill had my
attention.

I was surprised the little plane flew as well as it did. I decided to just fly on across the lake and land at my beach and winterize my cabin before going on down to Port Alsworth some nine miles away. When I got to PA, I left the plane there until I could get a little better fix on things and a calmer day to fly the pass on over to Soldotna for final repair.

CONCLUSION

I can say that I would not trade all these experiences for anything else; however, I would never care to undertake them again today. I am thankful to God for allowing me to go through them relatively injury free. By His grace I live to share with others and serve Him in the future in whatever capacity He wills.

I certainly don't believe God wants us to intentionally push the envelope. He creates us all with our own traits, likes, and dislikes. I for one had an inclination for adventure and pushing the envelope. Thankfully God had plans for my life that were far better than my earthly propensities might have allowed. In His graciousness He brought me through my trials and testing to set me on a path to serve Him better.

Today, I am honored to serve God under Samaritan Purse's Operation Heal Our Patriots (OHOP) far north program in remote Alaska, located in beautiful Port Alsworth. Under the founding and able leadership of Franklin Graham, the program honors many of America's wounded warrior couples in a setting of unsurpassed, pristine beauty so exemplary of God's marvelous creation.

Like a sentinel, a mountain stands just east of the town site and is often referred to as Holy Mountain—holey that is, not in a sacred sense, but as in full of holes. There are five of them. Four are very visible to the town site with a fifth one around on the south face, like a thumb print. It's as if God, after creating Earth, grasped this huge piece of granite like one would grasp a bowling ball and gave it a spin, causing the Earth's rotation to begin.

It is in this indescribable backdrop that I find myself blessed to bring to fruition my life's spirit of adventure. My prayer is that God will continue to use me for His honor and glory to the very end. The Apostle Paul, under the Inspiration of the Holy Spirit, aptly expressed it in his letter to the Church at Philippi:

"I press on to reach the end of the race and to receive the heavenly prize for which God, through Jesus Christ, is calling us" (Philippians 3:14, NLT).

Thank you for reading. If you enjoyed these real Alaskan adventures, you might look for my sequel. It will relate more wild tales of Alaskan bushmen and pilots. You don't want to miss it.

Review Inquiry

Hey, it's Ralph here.

I hope you've enjoyed the book, finding it both useful and fun. I have a favor to ask you.

Would you consider giving it a rating wherever you bought the book? Online book stores are more likely to promote a book when they feel good about its content, and reader reviews are a great barometer for a book's quality.

So please go to the website of wherever you bought the book, search for my name and the book title, and leave a review. If able, perhaps consider adding a picture of you holding the book. That increases the likelihood your review will be accepted!

Many thanks in advance,
Ralph Meloon, Jr.

WILL YOU SHARE THE LOVE?

Get this book for a friend, associate, or family member!

If you have found this book valuable and know others who would find it useful, consider buying them a copy as a gift. Special bulk discounts are available if you would like your whole team or organization to benefit from reading this. Just email ralphmeloon@gmail.com.

WOULD YOU LIKE RALPH MELOON, JR. TO SPEAK TO YOUR ORGANIZATION?

Book Ralph Now!

Ralph accepts a limited number of speaking engagements each year. To learn how you can bring his message to your organization, email ralphmeloon@gmail.com.

ABOUT THE AUTHOR

I was born a rebel, my grandfather on my mother's side was a rebel, and his father, my great grandfather, was a rebel who fought in the Civil War. We all had one thing in common: we despised the overreach of the Federal Government. That alone is a good reason I ended up escaping to Alaska to live out my life hunting, fishing, flying, and guiding. On my father's side were several generations of boat builders. This brought the family from Ossipee, New Hampshire to Orlando, Florida. The Confederate part of the family arrived from South Carolina. It was a match made in Heaven which culminated in me, Ralph Chester Meloon, Jr. being blessed to be born into a wonderful Christian home that honored and served God. My dad was Ralph C. Meloon Sr. and my mom was Betty R. Meloon.

A song written and sung by one of Alaska's most famous crooners, Hobo Jim (RIP), is "Wild and Free." Excerpts from its lyrics fit me to a tee: "There's a part of me, wild and free. In my heart there's a wild wolf howling through the tall pine trees . . . I can see that road spreading over the land, see a young boy standing with a suitcase in his hand. It was long ago, the boy was me. Got it in my mind that it must have been the time that caused me to wander away, from a family that I loved, and a warm roof above . . . didn't mind the hunger, the wind or the rain or the snow . . . I was on the road I wanted to be, just another man moving down the highway wild and free." I loved and lived that song, and until I answered the inner urging of my soul and headed off to Alaska for good, I was restless and unsatisfied. In the interim, I studied in several schools, peddled a bunch of boats, learned to fly an airplane, and headed off to The Great Land, Alaska. Along the way, I ended up with two wonderful families, including three beautiful and highly intelligent girls, Lisa, Tanya, and Heather (in that order age-wise), and a son, Jon. Today two of them live in Alaska and two in the lower 48. There are 11 grandchildren and 3 great grands, with one more on the way. As my late father used to always say, "Families are forever and are what matters, but God first."

Ralph can be reached at: ralphmeloon@gmail.com

www.ingramcontent.com/pod-product-compliance
Lightning Source LLC
Chambersburg PA
CBHW070712130626
46553CB00005B/1954